GOD AND ME

GOD AND ME

edited by
Candida Lund

THE THOMAS MORE PRESS
Chicago, Illinois

The short story, "The Gift"
Copyright © 1954 by Maureen Daly

Copyright © 1988 by the Thomas More Association. All
rights reserved. Printed in the United States of America.
No part of this publication may be reproduced, stored in
a retrieval system, or transmitted, in any form or by any
means, electronic, mechanical, photocopying, recording,
or otherwise, without the written permission of the publisher, The Thomas More Association, 223 W. Erie St.,
Chicago, Illinois 60610.

ISBN 0-88347-222-8

CONTENTS

PREFACE

"ALL happy families resemble one another, but each unhappy family is unhappy in its own way." The profundity (or is it absence thereof?) of those opening words of Tolstoy's *Anna Karenina* has always eluded me. Certainly, however, there is one relationship that each believing person has which, I assert, bears no resemblance to another's—one's relationship with God. Here, unquestionably, each such relationship is unique. This same position is held by at least one other person in this book, Bishop Norbert Gaughan. In his essay, "Me and God," he claims that "Each one has his own way of relating to God." That way may range from the passionate intensity of a Catherine of Siena to the winning insouciance of a Tevye in *Fiddler on the Roof*, but it is never the same as another's.

For the most part, this very private relationship is not one that people are disposed to speak about. Indeed, one could say that it would be difficult to find a subject upon which more of us are inarticulate. Hence, our greater indebtedness to the ten men and women in this book who have done so, never easily but with careful soul-searching.

Who are they? The mix includes a poet, a novelist, a bishop, a music critic, a doctor, a church historian, a college president, a journalist, an essayist, the head of a large Dominican congregation of women. Expectedly, each wears certain other hats as well, whether it be that of parent, teacher, feminist or theologian.

So much for the Who of the book. Why were they

9

chosen? Because as editor I recognized that each would have meaningful thoughts on this most mysterious of all subjects and would be able to express themselves. This book does not pretend to be encyclopedic; for one thing, only Christians are represented. This does not mean that it carries the Old Boys'/Old Girls' stamp. All connected with the book recognize that there are many mansions in God's house, just as they also recognize that there are growing numbers who lay no claim on God.

It has become chic in ever widening circles to claim to be almost godless. A doubt of the doubt often, however, seems to remain. This was caught by E.Y. Harburg in *Rhymes for the Irreverent* in a poem he entitled "Agnostic." His agnostic cannot "quite believe in God." He concludes, however,

> "But, oh I hope to God that He
> unswearvingly believes in me."

A note now for the reader's approach to this work. Many years ago Mortimer Adler wrote a helpful volume entitled *How to Read a Book*. I presume here to suggest how to, as well as how not to, read this book. Books can serve a variety of purposes, although not necessarily at the same time. Information. Encouragement. Inspiration. Enjoyment. A buttressing of one's own position. A stimulant to disputation.

It seems to me that for the reading of *God and Me* this last purpose should be ruled out. To dispute the way someone else relates to God is, I hold, a diminishment of one's own relationship with Him. One can say, "That is not the way it is for me" (bearing out my earlier assertion with respect to uniqueness), or even "This is not the way that I would want it to be for me," but denouncing is uncalled for.

Perhaps the best approach in reading these chapters is to follow the advice that the composer, Philip Glass, gave to a friend of mine when she expressed concern about going to see his opera, *Satyagraha*. He cautioned, "Sit back and let it happen."

So, read away and let it happen. You may be surprised!

Candida Lund
Rosary College
River Forest, IL

DEUS IN VITA MEA
(God in My Life)

Bernard J. Ransil

THE idea of writing about God's presence and influence in my life struck me as a congenial one at first: there would be a lot to say; I could almost write a book about it rather than a chapter. Now that I actually come to writing it—space cleared on the desk, sharpened pencils beside a pad of paper (the word processor does not seem a suitable instrument for such an undertaking)—I find myself deep in dilemma. What do I say about something that is the focus about which my life is organized, that gives meaning and direction to it, is as reflex as breathing and as elusive and private as thought? There is caution now where before there was candor. Go carefully, my instincts tell me, lest in writing about it, you undermine or depreciate it. For writing about something spiritual fixes in time and space something that is neither spatial nor temporal, thereby possibly distorting it. What is caught on paper is a fleeting glimpse of an underlying reality that changes as it is being written about, because it is being written about. If it is to be caught at all, it must be done so obliquely, by reflection, on the fly. It may not be recognizable a month or a year from now. At that distance it may appear to be naive, even foolish....

* * *

13

GOD AND ME

It seems as if I've always known about God. When I was a kid, he was part of life, like a piece of furniture in an old-fashioned parlor that one used on Sundays. I prayed to him in childish prayers of supplication as if he were Santa Claus and every day was Christmas. I was afraid of him because he knew what I was thinking and would punish me for copping cookies and hassling my sisters. I don't think I loved him because I didn't know what love was.

I went to a school where the entire enrollment of 400 kids sang the 8 o'clock mass every morning in Latin. So if you missed morning prayers, you made up for it at mass. I liked singing the mass with my schoolmates because everyone sang with an enthusiasm sometimes that made you feel something special was happening. And I liked learning new masses—which we did in the once-a-week music period, led by an *a capella* nun beating time with a rattan on a radiator. When you didn't have a piano, she would say, you used whatever God gave you, which told us something about both God and economics.

I particularly liked singing the Requiem, the mass for the dead, and when I got to be an altar boy, I particularly enjoyed censing the catafalque at the end of mass, and delighted in the billows of aromatic smoke that I, as number three altar boy, had the responsibility to generate. To fulfill this coveted duty, one rose discreetly from his knees immediately after consecration, genuflected devoutly, taking care not to trip over one's cassock (knowing that his classmates were watching him expectantly in the hope he would do so) and repaired quietly to a remote corner of the sacrisity where he lit a candle, took up a piece of char-

14

coal with a pair of tongs, lit its four corners and deposited it in the censer. He repeated this with two or three more pieces of charcoal then returned to his post at the altar, usually after all the "work" had been done, and the pastor had settled into the enigmatic and sonorous Gospel of St. John, "In the beginning was the Word and the Word was with God; and the Word was God."

As much as I liked the Requiem mass—less talk, more action—I liked a funeral mass even more, despite the sadness and at times the distressing grief of the occasion. Why was this? Because at the end of the mass and the prayers over the casket, the organist would sing *In Paradisum deducant te angeli* (May the angels lead thee into Paradise...), the simplest, purest, most lyrically tender farewell to a loved one there is, transporting me, perhaps not to Paradise, but close to it.

Being an altar boy meant several things—a certain prestige among one's classmates, occasional released time to practice for Forty Hours, the Easter week liturgy, or the well-attended Missions preached by the Redemptorists, a present at Christmas and a treat at the end of the school year—but above all it meant responsibility, the responsibility of showing up on time for each scheduled tour of duty.

The most difficult time to meet this responsibility was summer vacation. To serve the eight o'clock mass we had to get up at seven o'clock, which was our usual rising time during the school year. I hated getting up, especially if my brother, with whom I shared both room and bed, could remain luxuriously asleep. Occasionally we were scheduled to serve mass together, so we both had to get up, not particularly overjoyed to do so.

But once awake and on my way to church—a fifteen-minute walk through an Applachian woods that glittered with sun filtering through the brilliant green leaves, that glistened with dew sparkling like diamonds on grass and bushes—I was in love with the world: the birds that chattered and sang above me, the rabbits that skittered across the path ahead of me...and with God. Such moments happened only when I was alone, marching through the woods on my way to the altar of God where, to the opening prayer at the foot of the altar *Introibo ad altare Dei,* my partner and I would respond *Ad Deum qui laetificat juventutem meaum*—"I go unto the altar of God," "To God who giveth joy to my youth." Never were truer words spoken: there was much unconscious joy in my life those days, and God was a silent center and source of it.

One summer, my mother's father came to visit. He seemed very old and remote to us but he was kind and gentle, and went to mass every morning, walking through the woods with us when it was our turn to serve. He would speak to us in German-accented English which I had difficulty understanding. What I did understand about him, though, was that God was real to Grandpa, and that Grandpa loved him; God was his friend. The contact was brief, the impression—reinforced by subsequent history—permanent.

May and October were special months, not only because of the beauty of the woods during spring and fall, but because they were dedicated to Mary, which meant rosary, litany and benediction every Sunday, Wednesday and Friday evening at 7:30 PM. I attended these services habitually; always, because it was a welcome change from routine, and periodically, in the hope of getting a glimpse of, or maybe even saying a few words to, whichever classmate I happened to have a crush on at the time. (My single regret about these mixed motives is the wrong impression they may have created in the eyes of those who, in such behavior, saw evidence of a budding vocation.) But while thoughts of Virginia Mae or Ellen Francis or whoever perhaps got me to church those soft, mellow evenings, it was God who seemed to take over when I got inside. The rosary put me to sleep until I learned the trick of mediating on the particular event commemorated by each decade. Even when instructed in the technique of meditation by the nuns, it took time to learn, probably because it required the ability to meditate, to think abstractly, which for me developed only slowly. But then came the Litany of the Blessed Virgin Mary which I enjoyed for the cadenced rhythms of its inflected chants, and the responses that changed abruptly to new rhythmic patterns just as one was about to go into hypnotic trance.

Finally came the big moment, the exposition of the Blessed Sacrament in a golden monstrance, surrounded by seven-tiered candelabra, immersed in clouds of incense, accompanied by that most beautiful of hymns written by St. Thomas Aquinas, *O Salutaris Hostia*. There came a moment—like that described by the priest in Edwin O'Connor's *The Edge of Sadness*—of interior stillness, a

17

stillness deep inside in which there was an absence of all distraction, in which quietly and without effort I came together, focused, really present, a stillness in which it was natural, even inevitable to think of God, visible on the altar in the form of bread, to begin talking to him.

The fall also brought Forty Hours Devotion which was opened by a Solemn High Mass, followed by a procession in which the Blessed Sacrament, mounted in the monstrance, was carried under a canopy around the church. The procession included school children, the girls dressed all in white, the boys in navy blue pants, white shirts and Buster Brown collars, tied with large white satin cravats, each one carrying a large white pompom chrysanthemum. As we marched we sang hymns and chanted the Latin response to the Litany of Saints intoned by the pastor, resplendent in white vestments and billowing white cope. To one side, the assistant pastor, vested to match, censed the host. After circling the tiny basement church several times, the procession regained the altar and closed with Solemn Benediction.

Besides those special events there were low masses and high masses, masses for the dead, funerals and weddings— all with varying liturgies, with different music sung in Gregorian chant. Such diversity in liturgical ritual, in a language and musical form quite different from daily routine, injected a God-centered cultural influence into my life that leavened and enriched the pop culture in which I grew. Through such exposure I not only developed an interest in learning foreign languages and a taste for classical music, but God became tangible and real. And

Bernard J. Ransil

I learned I could talk to him as I might, say, to the parish priest, to my teachers, to mother and grandma, to a father. But not to my own father, who never learned to reconcile his disciplinary responsibilities, which he took very seriously, with expressing his love for us. He could never just. . . talk to us. When he spoke, Authority spoke, and the knees trembled and the heart went through a series of hemi-demi-semi quavers that registered 6.3 on the Richter scale.

Such were my childhood experiences of God: catechism and religion classes where I learned *about* him at a level appropriate to my ability to think abstractly; a rich liturgy and formal prayer through which I began to feel his presence and learned to talk to him.

But, looking back, I now realize the talk was the inconsequential chatter of a child, the innocent prattle of a happy youngster in the company of someone he trusts. I didn't really think of God as a being with whom I could have a personal relationship as with my friends and family, but he was still someone I thought of when I prayed, and to whom I spoke when I said the "Our Father." I just took him for granted as part of the environment in which I lived. I didn't really begin to think about him critically until high school. It happened this way.

Electing to go to a Catholic high school rather than attend the local public school two miles away (walking distance in those days), I discovered that my options were two parish high schools that were two streetcars and forty-five minutes away if one was lucky enough in connections. I chose the one with the better academic reputation—St. Mary of the Mount, taught by the Immaculate Heart nuns

19

whose motherhouse was in Scranton, Pennsylvania. I chose it because its core academic curriculum consisted of four years each of religion, mathematics, English and Latin, three years of science (biology, chemistry and physics), two years of history, one year of civics. There were miscellaneous courses like typing and library research skills, and activities like class plays, orchestra, glee club, newspaper and yearbook. But no sports. Back then sports was something one did at home, with one's playmates, in one's neighborhood. It didn't intrude on the school curriculum because one went to school to learn a systematic body of knowledge that one could not get at home or from the pop culture. And if one wanted to learn about God as well, he went to a parochial school.

From the vantage point of hindsight informed by subsequent education and teaching at four institutions of higher learning, I now see that the nuns who taught me, both at my parish grade school and at St. Mary's, were a remarkable group of women. They were first and foremost real, three-dimensional people who radiated common sense and an enthusiasm for their work. God was part of their lives and they made him part of ours. They knew who they were, what they were about. They were personally involved with each of their students. And they enjoyed teaching because I enjoyed learning from them. I was a perpetually dry sponge and they were an infinite sea of knowledge and culture.

Many classes at St. Mary's, especially the humanities, were taught combining lecture and discussion group techniques. And God was integrated into the curriculum when-

Bernard J. Ransil

ever reference to him was relevant and appropriate. Religion was...not so much taught as...discussed, using as a springboard a four-volume paperback work called, *A Course in Religion for Catholic High Schools and Academies*, written by a church historian, Rev. John Laux, published by Benziger Brothers. Each volume contained material enough for one academic year and took up in turn the basic tenets of the Christian faith, and their biblical and historical sources; the sacraments, the mass, sacramentals and indulgences; general and special morality—a year long intensive course in ethics; and the rational basis for belief in God, in Christ and the Church.

If the fundamental act of religion is a conscious turning to God—or conversion, as some say it is—then my turning to God as a consciously convinced Christian, my conscious conversion, occurred slowly and imperceptibly during the fourth year religion class at St. Mary's. This class—on the reasonableness of belief of such things as the existence of God, the immortality of the soul, the divinity of Christ and infallibility—was conducted in the discussion group mode mentioned earlier. As homework, we would be assigned a coherent section from Laux which would include the author's text plus perhaps material quoted from the Bible, the Church Fathers, Newman and Aquinas. Calling the class to order, the nun would review the day's assignment in case we had missed the point or hadn't read the material, then would move to the side of the room whence she would open the discussion with a provocative question guaranteed to get the ball rolling. "Mary Lois, what do you think of infallibility?" If there was an

21

heretical point of view possible or an unusual exegesis, Mary Lois could be counted on to come up with it and to get everyone else caught up in (sometimes clamorous) discussion.

From that point on, fifty minutes sped by in continuous questions and discussion about what we had read, what it meant, was it reasonable to believe, and so on. Every heresy that ever arose in history concerning God, Christ and the Church was exhumed in those classroom sessions, discussed and reconciled with reason through the strength of the material and the skill of the nun-moderator. Through such systematic discourse, through the patience and tact of a fine teacher, what my soul knew years earlier came to be seen and accepted by my intellect. What faith had known instinctively, the intellect now knew from reason. I had reached the age of reason and my faith was buttressed, rather than shattered, by it.

But in the course of absorbing and discussing the biblical, theological, historical and exegetical material presented in those religion classes, my knowledge of God and of his creation had changed dramatically and irreversibly. My anthropomorphic concepts of him—as a kind of paternal father figure who kept score of my transgressions—had been absorbed and replaced by the concept of a pure spirit who had indirectly communicated with mankind through the Old Testament Prophets and directly through his Son. It seemed more natural now, because I was human and because he had taken human form and had lived a human life, to relate to God as Jesus, which the doctrine of the Trinity made easy, without violation of logic or loyalties:

they were one and the same, but distinct. Nevertheless, although it was easier to relate to the historical person, Jesus, than to the pure spirit God, I never lost the sense that I was talking to God the pure spirit, as I talked to Christ the God-become-man; just as I knew I was talking to Christ, present in the form of bread, when I talked to the Eucharist.

This extensive metamorphosis of my religious beliefs resulted in a better understanding of what they meant and a stronger conviction of their essential credibility. And with that came the gradual realization that I should put these beliefs into practice. It was an easy course to chart, but a difficult one to implement, for such an undertaking takes persistent patience and will power, both of which were in short supply. (The will, I was to discover, resembled a muscular organ: it got strong when it was exercised; it got flabby when it was not.) Nevertheless I set about consciously integrating my belief in God and its implications into my life, a decision that was to open many doors, close a few, and prove an important factor in many major decisions in my life.

At the center of this belief, illuminating and vitalizing it, was God. I was a human being created by him, created in his image. I came into this world, a collection of genes infused with an immortal soul, deposited in an environment from which I drew sustenance and support, not knowing who or what I was. My identity was inextricably linked with that image of God in which I had been created. My search for identity was to be a search for that image. The quickest way, the only way, then, to discover who

GOD AND ME

I was, was to learn what God's will for me was, and to do it. And the quickest way to do that was to go to him directly. (I had not developed the habit of praying to Mary for her intercession with God because God was as approachable as any friend. I had never gone through a friend's mother when I wanted to enlist a friend's help, so it didn't seem natural somehow to do it with God. On the other hand, prayer in appreciation and praise of Mary was as natural as telling a friend what a great person his mother was.) Increasingly I found myself saying, in moments of silent communion snatched between activities, at morning on rising, at night before falling asleep: "Lord, what is your will for me?" "Lord, let me know your will that I may do it." "Lord, tell me what you want me to do and give me the energy to do it."

One such decision concerned a vocation to the priesthood. A young man raised at the time and in the culture I was, couldn't escape at least considering the possibility: the expectation was always there, implied, if not spoken. I never thought much about it until my college years when the pressure for a career decision became persistent and uncomfortable. I couldn't make such a decision at the time with any degree of confidence because I did not know who I was, what I could do or what I wanted to do. I knew of only one strategy—to follow up on the areas of study I liked and discard those I didn't. The strategy didn't work because I enjoyed everything I had studied in college (science, philosophy, music, mathematics, languages, literature) and wanted to continue developing them all. When I prayed for illumination, for direction, I sensed only one

Bernard J. Ransil

response: keep your options open; do not close any doors unnecessarily.

Complicating the situation was the publication of Thomas Merton's *Seven Storey Mountain* and later his *Seeds of Contemplation.* The former was a literary sensation and a runaway best seller. Suddenly, hundreds if not thousands of young Catholic men, influenced by the persuasive appeal of the book, the uncertainty of the world situation (the Korean War) and the draft, were entering monasteries and seminaries all over the country. My college friends and I did not escape this tidal wave that tugged at the heart, mind and soul and...offered refuge in a mixed-up world. We read, talked, prayed and privately debated the decision. I was on the fence and prayer gave me no answers. But prayer *had* steered me to a more direct and unambiguous form of communication with God—a spiritual director, who eventually asked the decisive question. Referring to the vow of obedience one day he asked, "Do you want someone else to make the critical decisions in your life?" The answer was immediate and instinctive: I did not see God's will for me in the will of a religious superior; I did not have a vocation to the priesthood. The immense relief I experienced was as sudden, startling and illuminating as a bolt of lightning, and the self-knowledge it conveyed rolled like thunder. I had learned one very important negative piece of information about myself that was as valuable as any positive piece of information. One door was closed, but a seeming infinity of doors stood open before me.

In choosing a college, graduate and professional school,

25

the God-factor was as important as location, cost and quality of curriculum, facilities and faculty. The choice of university was limited by circumstances (in which I saw the operation of God's will) to a local Catholic university with a solid reputation for teaching but not research. It combined what I wanted at the time with what was possible. It turned out to be exactly what I needed at that stage of development. If I had gone to an ivy league school, I jokingly remarked to a friend many years later, I would probably have lost my faith, my morals and my marbles. Not because those environments necessarily affected one that way (Bill Buckley survived Yale after all) but because they offered options and opportunities that I was not then wise enough in the ways of the world to handle.

The selection of a graduate school for a Ph.D. in physical chemistry was a different matter because the choice lay between three top ranking secular universities and the two Catholic universities, at the time, which had the best chemistry departments. Here, the fact that Catholic University in Washington, D.C., was Catholic and had an exceptional physical chemistry department decided the issue. The choice of the University of Chicago for medical school was congenial and natural for many reasons, not the least of which was that it was a campus animated by religious humanism, with a very active Catholic student center, and that it had already been home for some time.

And so it happened that I acquired my university, graduate school and professional education at institutions where God lived on campus and was part of the scholarly curriculum. Institutions where one could attend philosophy

Bernard J. Ransil

lectures and lectures in theology and religion of a caliber
commensurate with one's secular education—lectures that
met one's intellectual and spiritual needs and supported
one's scholarly goals; where there was a spiritual ferment
that enlivened and gave meaning and direction to the intense intellectual exercise; where there was an opportunity to meet others with similar interests, values and beliefs.

As my religious beliefs slowly became incorporated into my life, God increasingly became a part of my friend-
ships, my lifestyle and my work. I will not write of my
friends and family members who are living, who have been
the salt, the leaven of my life, the source of much spontaneous joy, the stimulus for much intellectual, emotional
and spiritual growth. But I can write of Joan Lou who remains in the memory as if etched in granite because she
spoke of God so often and so unself-consciously, as if he
were a member of the family, a close friend, a confidante,
an advisor, a mentor, a spiritual director. Clearly he *was*
all these things to her and, as we became acquainted and
then firm friends at Catholic University, she enabled me
to perceive and meet God on the same terms. Joan Lou
married, brought up a family and died in her prime of sys-
temic lupus erythematosis. Throughout all this she remained a constant friend, forever on the same frequency,
a desultory correspondent, an avid bridge player and
reader of mysteries, a sympathetic and supportive listener
via Ma Bell, a direct pipeline to God. If heaven has the
equivalent of a bridge tournament, she is probably running it, a cigarette in one hand, a Beefeaters-on-the-rocks
in the other. She loved God in a personal way that was

27

infectious. Having known God through faith from early childhood, then through reason from high school, Joan Lou taught me to know him through the emotions. I mourned Joan Lou when she died, but her death only seemed to make God more accessible.

And I can speak of Father Jerome, a priest-psychiatrist and English Benedictine who for over twenty years was friend, spiritual director and confessor as I shuttled back and forth between Washington, D.C., Chicago and Boston on various research projects. After meeting at Catholic University and staying in frequent contact during my years at Chicago, we converged on Boston where he was establishing an institute for patient care, teaching and research in psychiatry, within several years of each other. During our biweekly meetings at St. Anselm's Priory in Washington, we discussed the wide range of subjects spanning our interests, including the disciplines of psychology and psychiatry.

Those were the days when what appeared to be an attempt by "secular" psychiatry to assume the spiritual functions of prayer and confession were widely discussed in the religious and secular press and in such books as Joshua Loth Liebman's *Peace of Mind* and Fulton J. Sheen's response, *Peace of Soul*. Father Jerome's views on these controversies were sensible and reassuring. Where the psychiatric disorders were functional or organic-functional in etiology, he felt that "secular" psychiatry was appropriate. However, if there was a spiritual component to the disorder arising from the intimate relationship between soul and intellect, then neither psychiatric theory nor treatment would suffice: The patient's spiritual life, his relationship between self and God, also must be included in the therapeutic plan. A psychiatrist who did not believe in a personal God was ill-equipped to do this. At the same time, a priest or rabbi was as ill-equipped to cope with the psychiatric side of things. Father recognized the dilemma and attempted to answer it by establishing a center for psychiatric treatment, teaching and research that included the spiritual dimension. Father's practice attracted priests and nuns from all over the country and, I think, broke new ground. But he never found the time to publish extensively and the institute lost its religious orientation when he died.

If Joan Lou taught me to know God through the emotions, Father Jerome taught me to look for a God-relationship gone awry in the diagnosis and treatment of mental and emotional disorders. It was an orientation that served me well when, as a medical student at the University of Chicago and as part of Chicago's standard medical school curriculum at the time, I received four years intensive training and patient care experience in psychiatry. A measure of the growth, at the time, in my knowledge of the structure and function of the human body was that, whereas in the past *Mens sana in corpore sano* ("A healthy mind in a healthy body") had been my therapeutic ideal, my horizons had now expanded to include soul and emotions with mind and body as therapeutic concerns.

But my concerns were not limited to the realm of therapeutics. The knowledge I had gained of how these four components of the human person—body, mind, soul and emotions—depended upon one another, and interacted with one another, spilled over into my personal life and began to direct and regulate it. My perception of the human body and its function had been radically altered by medical school. As a child I had learned that the body was the temple of the Holy Ghost, which metaphor, while generating a desirable respect for the body, at the same time attributed to it an undesirable sacred character that tended to discourage, if not prohibit, its legitimate and rational study. On the other hand, the body was not a thing to be taken for granted, treated casually, abused unthinkingly. It was the organism upon which, for as long as I lived, the health, integrity and development of the mind, emotions and soul depended. It needed proper care—hygiene, nourishment, shelter, protection from injury, medical treatment—in order to survive and thrive. While the gratification of its appetites was pleasurable and could be enjoyed, it must be regulated by the knowledge that the appetites are signals that certain physiological needs be met, not playtoys or relief valves for aggression, depression and boredom. Failure to take care of the organism and habitual abuse of its appetites compromised it, resulting in physical, mental and emotional disability and illness, and possibly death. I had, of course, always known that eating and drinking to excess, smoking and sexual promiscuity, for example, were "bad" for the body, but medical training drove the point home as only first-hand experience can do, with my psychiatric training making the same point for the mind and emotions.

The year spent on Christian morals and ethics in high school prepared me for the many perplexing moral dilem-

Bernard J. Ransil

mas I encountered in medicine and provided an excellent foundation upon which to think about and formulate principles concerning what was morally acceptable and unacceptable in medical research and in the diagnosis and treatment of human disorders and disease. But whereas in the past, my criteria for making moral judgements had been derived primarily from Divine Law, as interpreted by the Church, my medical training taught me that God's will concerning moral judgements with respect to biomedical phenomena could also in part be inferred from the nature of the phenomena themselves, which we could learn about through research.

Sexual promiscuity, for example, was morally wrong, not only because the sixth and ninth commandments (broadly interpreted) forbade it, but because epidemiological studies clearly demonstrated that it generated disease and disseminated it. It violated the well-being of human beings whom God had created, and worked against their best interests, rather than promoting them. So these two commandments in reality were guidelines, or warning signals, to help mankind avoid making a serious mistake.

All of the commandments could be seen in this light, I realized, as rules that promote the well-being of the individual and society, of all creation, which is God's will for creation, from which desideratum the commandments derive their authority. One obeys the Commandments, not because God or the Church demands it, but because they protect us from behavior which undermines our nature, which if practiced habitually will disable and destroy us.

31

In other words, moral law is at the service of mankind, not the other way around (just as "The Sabbath was made for man, not man for the Sabbath"), as many people mistakenly believe, in impulsively reacting against it. Morality is often viewed as a series of Thou-shalt-nots rather than as the detailed prescription for implementing "Thou shalt love the Lord thy God with thy whole heart and with thy whole soul and with thy whole mind. Thou shalt love thy neighbor as thyself." For if one loves one's self properly, he takes proper care of his body, regulating its appetites to conform to its physiological needs, exercising it to maintain its integrity of function, protecting it from injury and disease, thus enabling it to support and implement the activities of the mind and soul. And if one loves his neighbor, he not only does not aggress upon him (that is, observe the "Thou-shalt-nots") but loves his neighbor as himself.

If the commandments and the moral law protect us from behavior which undermines human nature and human values, then the obverse of that coin is that sin is the condition of knowingly and habitually disregarding those rules, behaving in a manner that is inconsistent with our welfare and the welfare of created things. As a consequence of this association, sin may be recognized by its effects on the person, just like disease may be recognized by its symptoms ("By their fruits ye shall know them."): it undermines human values and disables and destroys human lives and created things. The classic "seven capital sins" are nothing but a catalogue of the symptoms of sin: pride, covetousness, lust, anger, gluttony, envy and sloth. There are, of course, many more. In such matters, as with technology, man is very inventive.

Bernard J. Ransil

These considerations gradually led me to think about research as a mechanism by which God communicates to mankind about created things, rather than as a secular force often at odds with the doctrines of religion. The notion of God communicating his will to mankind through the medium of created things, with reason (and therefore scholarship and research) as the means by which mankind attains the knowledge God wishes to communicate, is not new—it's called Natural Revelation. But identifying scholarship and research as instruments of Natural Revelation, with Natural Revelation dependent on them for detailed information on the structure and function of created things, if not new, at least does not seem to be explicitly recognized by the Church when evaluating the morality of research and research applications, especially in the domain of biomedical phenomena.

If God is communicating to us through our knowledge of created things, and I believe he is, then I would expect what we learn and infer from research about human nature to be compatible with what we learn and infer from Divine Revelation. However, I do not find this to be so.

In the areas of human sexuality and reproduction, for example, I observe a profound difference of opinion concerning the morality of research in these fields and its applications, between the people who actually study the phenomena and produce the information about them (i.e., those who are generating the data from created things which contain the message God wishes to communicate to us), and the magisterium of the Church (i.e., those who infer and interpret God's will from Scripture and tradition). The difference of opinion arises from fundamental-

33

ly different ways of looking at the nature and origins of human life.

One group (which for lack of a better term, and with apologies, I will call the "secular scientists") view the human being as a living organism animated by a vital principle, composed of many organs, capable of many functions. While these individuals can address and answer questions about the structure of the human being, including its mind and emotions, they can say nothing about the nature of the animating life principle other than that such a principle exists and that its locus appears to be in the pacemaker region of the heart. The other group, comprising the magisterium of the Church and (often) a consulting body made up of theologians and other scientists (whom I shall distinguish as "religious scientists") appears to agree with this viewpoint in all respects except that it proceeds to define the nature of the animating vital principle as the immortal human soul infused by God at conception.

At this point, the two groups part company, not necessarily because the definition is unacceptable to the first, but because of its implications concerning human origins and the nature of human life. In the eyes of the contemporary Church, possession of the immortal soul sets human life apart from all other forms of created life, and confers on it an absolute sanctity that preempts all other considerations when making moral judgements, even if those judgements seem to be inconsistent with the knowledge about human sexuality and reproduction gained from human experience and research. The secular scientists, from their intimate knowledge of the human organism and of human

Bernard J. Ransil

reproduction know that, while human life has a unique value that must be defended and respected, at the same time this value, by its very nature, is not absolute. Nature is demonstrably profligate with human life, especially with the early forms of prenatal life. (An example of what I have in mind is given a little later.) But the believer knows that God created Nature and that it works according to his design. Should man therefore accept as absolute what Nature (God) apparently does not?

At another level, should what God is telling us through Divine Revelation contradict what he is telling us through Natural Revelation? I do not think so. There has to be some underlying unifying principle that reconciles these diverse points of view. I think that principle is the fact that God is communicating with us through both media and that there can be no contradiction in what he is trying to tell us.

I can detect God's will in both viewpoints just as I see it on both sides of the debates in physics and biology that arose in the nineteenth century and spilled over into the early part of the twentieth. Those debates were triggered off by new information and theories in the physical and biological sciences that appeared to contradict certain religious doctrines. The resulting conflict produced an abrasive dialectic that ultimately resulted in a beneficial clarification of religious doctrine and of the limits of science. Those conflicts never arise in mainstream science and religion nowadays because they are no longer relevant; they have been resolved in a manner that is consistent with what is known about the physical world as God created it.

When I think about those obsolete quarrels, I think of

GOD AND ME

Santayana's oft-quoted and as often misquoted aphorism: "Those who cannot remember the past are condemned to repeat it" and wonder: Is the Church in the same predicament concerning her interpretation of created things that she was over a century ago? If so, can she not benefit from that experience?

That God is communicating to us about human sexuality and reproduction in both Divine Revelation and in the research being done on it, I have no doubt. That we are listening, especially to what research and human experience (the sources of Natural Revelation) have to say, I am not sure. I am not sure because in reading the magisterium's communcations on such matters, there is no evidence that the authors have had any practical experience or exposure to the phenomena they are writing about. For example, the recent "Instruction on Respect for Human Life in Its Origin and on the Diginity of Procreation" issued by the Congregation for the Doctrine of the Faith contains no documentary evidence that sources other than previous Popes' writings on sexual and marital matters have been consulted. I am not sure because attempting to understand God's will about created things only on the basis of Divine Revelation has, in the past, led the Church into serious doctrinal difficulties, e.g., the literal interpretation of Creation, the Galileo case. I am not sure because the outcome of such unilateral scholarship are positions that do not seem to harmonize with what we know about created things. A few examples will serve to illustrate the point.

The contemporary Church teaches that God infuses the immortal human soul at conception. This should be evaluated against the following. There is no Scriptural basis for this teaching, and tradition is not helpful. The teaching is contradicted by St. Thomas' theory of ensoulment which is firmly rooted in, and consistent with, an essentially correct knowledge of prenatal life development. Millions of fertilized eggs are spontaneously aborted by natural mechanisms in the world every day. For each fertilized egg that reaches term, millions of others are destroyed. Such wholesale slaughter of "human beings" as the Church calls them would suggest that Nature (which God created and designed) does not have the same "sense" of absolute "sanctity" of each fertilized egg or embryo as does the Church which, in the Instruction cited above, teaches that "From the moment of conception, the life of every human being (sic) is to be respected in an absolute way.... "Human life is sacred.... "

Every physical system is limited. The planet Earth, while vast, still has only a limited amount of space and a limited amount of natural resources to support mankind in a manner that will enable each person to fulfill God's will for him/her. On the other hand, human population, unchecked by war, flood, famine, pestilence or technology, is growing exponentially. Can an indefinitely expanding population on a finite planet be God's will for his creation? I do not think so because it is unreasonable. In principle, it must be God's will that the human population be limited at some point in time not only because of natural physical constraints, but to provide each person sufficient environmental support to work out his/her salvation. Is the Church's teaching on population control at the personal level compatible with the physical realities of population control at the global level?

If sin undermines human values and works against the welfare of the human race, as for instance, sexual promiscuity does, then we would expect the practice of contraception to have an adverse effect on the couples and marriages that use it. But such is not the case. There are hundreds of thousands of healthy and holy marriages in which rational contraceptive techniques have been routinely practiced.

In each of these controversies, the Church looks at each issue primarily from the viewpoint of Divine Revelation and faith, as interpreted by herself, whereas her opposition is coming from the world of human experience and knowledge of created things, i.e., from the domain of Natural Revelation, with information that should be complementary, not contradictory. Where religion seems to be pitted against science, and the teaching derived from Divine Revelation appears to conflict with the data of Natural Revelation, my personal sense of the situation is that God is speaking to us through both media. He is present on both sides of such controversies but unless we look for him in both media, he and what he wishes to communicate to us will be overlooked.

Religious doctrine has evolved over the centuries from the deposit of truth contained in Scripture and tradition. However, God continues to communicate to mankind through research, scholarship and human experience. Religious doctrine must therefore remain open to this continuing source of Revelation and must be compatible with

Bernard J. Ransil

what we learn from it, if it is to reflect God's will for mankind in the world he designed and created.

* * *

Thus it goes with God and me. He is there, present in the core of his creation, not to be seen directly, but indirectly, ricocheting off created things and seen by reflection in the lives of people, in the design of created things. As one lives with a sense of God's presence in created things and attempts to translate this sense into everyday life, he finds himself looking for God in people; for God's design in Nature; and his life is never again the same.

ME AND GOD

Norbert F. Gaughan

IT'S very personal to talk about "Me and God." It's almost as personal as (and possibly more personal than) a husband's speaking about the way he and wife relate, how they love and share their intimate thoughts. The exercise is not something that one should do easily, for it is not a process that is common to all. Each one has his own way of relating to God. It's similar to a love affair which, if exposed to the public light, may result in a change in the relationship.

Notice that the topic is "Me and God"—not "God and Me." Protocol or a recognition of God's superiority and status might indicate otherwise. "Me and God"—it's not that the "me" is first because it's most important, but because it's the "me" who relates only one person's dealings with God. The results can be very subjective. It certainly includes the possibility that the tale will not be of much help to anybody else except purely as a matter of curiosity. "Me and God" can be a record of the idiosyncrasies of the "me" versus the stability and permanence of the God.

The classic example of "Me and God" is St. Augustine's *Confessions,* the best seller of the early Middle Ages. It's still a classic, for the saint is not afraid to let himself go in an intimate dialogue with the God he loves and whom

Norbert F. Gaughan

he pursued with utmost love. His use of the personal pronoun does not jar. After all, he comes to us as a certified saint (even if he was also a reformed sinner). There are quotes galore which have become staples in Catholic teaching. "Late have I loved thee," the saint says to God, and still more.

However, in the following, the author reflects upon the "me" in the third person, lest the personal pronoun become wearisome. This does not diminish its sincerity: it is more a sketch of the author in his search for God's presence and meaning in his life.

As a boy, he sat often in his parish church, gazing up to the ceiling. There, covering the central area, was a painting done by a church decorator depicting the Blessed Trinity. It was done in the form of a large circle. Dominant was the figure of an old man with long flowing hair and a white beard. The face was severe and stood out in contrast to the flowing robes in which he was clothed. To his right was a young man with a brown beard, so positioned that it seemed as if his hand were on the shoulder of the patriarch. To the left, suspended in air, was a great white bird which later the young boy discovered was a representation of a dove.

But dominant was the old patriarch—stern, not quite like anything the boy had ever seen. No one told him—he picked it up almost by osmosis—that this was a representation of the Blessed Trinity. (Are there any such paintings in the new churches? Not many. They seem to have disappeared in favor of resurrected and smiling Christs, or the Jesus of the football field, with arms thrown upward as if he had just scored a touchdown.) The dove was the Spririt, and the young man, of course, Christ. And down through the years, the dove and the young man became almost obliterated from memory. But all his life, he would remember that central figure who he was told, after asking, was God the Father.

That's how the author's acquaintance with God began. It became an image which throughout his life he had to mend, correct and counterbalance by the other things he discovered about the Son and the Spirit. There's another image that haunts this man the young boy came to be. Seated in that church (which never really was a church but a converted large hall which had belonged to a male choral society), the youth had much time to study that image, as he was in the church for daily Mass. (Those were the times when the Catholic school child always began the school day with Mass.) As this was the parish church, it had its own organist who also did the singing during Mass. The organist, whose flair was for the dramatic and the full diapason, accentuated, or so it seemed, certain parts of the Mass. It created, at least in the Catholic boy, a sense that what was taking place was out of the ordinary, something unusual, even dramatic.

Thus the boy's life became a pursuit. No, not in search of the dominant patriarchal figure painted on the ceiling of his parish church, but a desire to discover the other faces of God. In a sense, it was a search not only for another face of God as a corrective on the haunting image of the Father as depicted, but to discover some other places where God might be and where he might be found.

Norbert F. Gaughan

Odd how little this one remembers of his grade school education. Instances stand out, a memory here and there. He was raised in a traditional Catholic home, a product of two cultures (the Irish of the father and the Polish of the mother). The Catholic faith was more absorbed than taught. Growing into adolescence, he follows the family's Catholic path. Every time the Pope meets this priest (it's not that many times), when the pontiff learns that this bishop with an Irish name speaks the Polish language, he immediately tells those around him how the mother is definitely the keeper of the culture. In a way his mother did do that, stressing also the Irish heritage. Strong Catholicity was a part of both cultures.

The youth remembers being taken off to the "Irish" church by the father on certain rare Sundays (which involved a treat at a soda fountain on the way home). At the "Irish" church, the ambiance was quite different. That pastor was enterprising in enticing people from other congregations to attend. So, for example, there is the memory of a Mass at Christmas in which there was a live creche in which the infant Jesus cried continually and became a nuisance. Did that image drive home the humanity of Jesus? Why is that scene remembered? It wasn't the issue, but it did make the point that Christmas really happened and involved live (i.e. real) humans.

The young student went off to high school. When he entered the Central Catholic High School of Pittsburgh, he had to learn all the "official" prayers in English. For some reason or other, he hadn't been taught them at the Polish elementary school. He had new English hymns (so

different from the Polish ones), and set his face to his
goal—to do at some altar some day what his pastor had
done surrounded by that music he had heard every day
when young before classes started.

Was his desire to become a priest a pursuit of God? It's
hard to say. It was something that he wanted, and the only
goal he sought to achieve. Perhaps the first stage in finding another face of God happened through the philosophy
courses he took in the seminary. There he came to study
the God of philosophy, a project verified by no less than
Thomas Aquinas and the spokesmen for him in this day,
Jacques Maritain and Etienne Gilson. Even if the studies
were academic, yet there was an appeal. Gilson became
the favorite author to be consulted about the God of the
philosophers. The student was quite delighted to learn how
Thomas Aquinas identified the God who spoke to Moses
through the burning bush with the God of philosophy and
theology of that day. He noted particularly that this God
of philosophy was not (for him) some sterile, abstract concept, but was responsible for the existence of all that was,
for everything that existed (even stones and mountains and
greenery), for everything that had life or shared in "existence."

Admittedly, to this student who later became a priest,
no small part of his calling and his work in daily life, was
the notion that the God of Being, the *God Who Is,* was
responsible for everything else. He became quite content
with the notion that Jesus who, according to St. John's
Gospel, said in the temple to those who were persecuting
him, "Before Abraham was, I am", thereby identified

44

Norbert F. Gaughan

himself with the God of Moses, who was further seen as the God of philosophy, the God of Being, the God Who Is.

Now the emphasis on "God, the Son" was directed to the young man who was painted standing at the side of the patriarch in that picture on the ceiling of the parish church. The student understood that who this person, the Son, was, was not an easily given answer. But it was this Jesus who had said, "He who sees me, sees the Father." It occurred to the seminarian there was no better way to see Jesus and the Father than to be God's minister at the altar, and to speak in sermons about him, to help others discover the accessibility of God through Jesus.

About ten years after his ordination, a strange thing happened to the young priest. Father Andrew Greeley has said that in every Catholic there is the potential for mysticism. It wasn't anything like a mystical experience, but, about the age of 35, something happened to the priest's perceptions of the world. He was made aware of the many and varied colors in the created world. It's not easily explained. If any personal mystical experience, says William James, is "ineffable," even if this was a minor event, it altered something in his understanding.

This change in the perception of the world might have been an outcome of the understanding that God is the God of creation, of all that is. He had a heightened intensity of the varieties of color in the universe, and it was almost like a kind of conversion. He became more aware of the diversity of all of God's creatures: the flowers, fields, mountains, seas. For him, creation indeed was revealed as a many hued matter. It may have had something to do with his whilom pursuit, photography, but whatever it was, it reiterated the grandeur of God, and also his many revelations of himself.

It may have been the influence of reading too much of St. Augustine. In his *Confessions*, the saint wrote: "But what do I love when I love Thee? Not the beauty of the body, not the fair adornment of time, not the bright light so dear to these eyes, not the sweet melodies of all kinds of song, not the sweet scent of flowers, unguents, and spices, not manna nor honey, not limbs pleasant to the embraces of the flesh. Not these do I love, when I love my God. And yet there is a light, a song, a fragrance, a food, an embrace, which I love when I love my God—the light, song, fragrance, food, and embrace of my inner man, where there shines in my soul that which no place contains, where there sounds that which time bears not away, where there is a fragrance which the breeze does not disperse, a taste which no greed makes less, and an embrace which no satiety puts asunder. This it is that I love, when I love my God."

Part of the priest's intellectual pursuits were due to a philosophy teacher he had in the seminary. He was a Benedictine monk who had great sympathy for the Neo-Platonic tradition passed along through Augustine in Church teaching. Lest this be too academic, what was understood was that God is revealed, as the Letter to the Romans says, in his creation. "Since the creation of the world, invisible realities, God's eternal power and divinity, have become visible, recognized through the things he has made."

So the priest began his personal celebration of the hidden multiformity of God in all the places he could be found in creation's color. Behind the colors was the multiformity. His personal celebration, begun long before Vatican II, prompted this author to search for the faces of God to be revealed in the things he made.

As the young priest in a parish, the priest discovered that he had some free time, so he decided on his own (without ecclesiastical support or finances) to pursue further studies at a secular university—the University of Pittsburgh— which was close by. It was not really a deliberate, conscious choice (i.e. as a stage on a journey to a definite goal). Upon reflection, he sometimes opines it could have been the hand of God leading him as he wandered into the philosophy department (which was highly regarded across the country). There he began to hear different tongues and discovered the words and ideas of others after Thomas Aquinas, who also had some things to say about God, even indirectly.

This reflection upon "Me and God" is not meant to be a story of vocation. Yet to this day he is convinced that a providential God arranged it all. In his spare time and on his days off he was able, after a time, to earn a degree of Doctor of Philosophy, which really meant he had his visions of God reinforced, tempered, emended by the thoughts and views of the modern philosophers, especially those in vogue then, the existentialists.

While the priest's life was bound up in many clerical duties, he found some satisfaction and even joy in being available for people who needed to talk about their experiences with God. He was stationed in a small town near the mountains in Western Pennsylvania, where he sought to discover God's nearness in the valleys, in the vistas, in the peace and the tranquility of the forests and woods. These exercises were never a flight from humanity, yet they became as much as a place for the person to re-create, be reinforced, and to learn that most mysterious fact that one can find God *also* in quiet and solitude.

Was his priestly life in any way a search to be in touch with God? He hoped so. This priest, as most priests, found that love of God is reflected in the people who are parishioners, who do generous things for their children, their families and neighbors. They have such a trusting faith in God. These were Catholics who, even though they had given sons to the wars, and had themselves sacrificed in hard times, never lost that trust.

But he was removed from parish life to become a "white collar worker" in an office. This was a different way to look for God, to find that *deus absconditus*, the hidden God. One day, after many years working in the Chancery, he prayed, "Lord, send me a cross." But he looked around his surroundings, the dull, uneventful and people-less activities of the office, and concluded that indeed he already had one!

Meanwhile the priest also looked for God in his reading. Somewhere about this time, he came across a book by the late John Courtney Murray. He had read much by the Jesuit who had contributed some great insights into the question of Church and State. But this was a different work, a slim volume, *The Problem of God Yesterday and Today*. It was an apparent departure for the Jesuit theologian and consisted of lectures he had given at a secular university. Murray wanted to demonstrate how throughout history there have been different names and definitions of God. First he discussed the definition in the Old Testament, as God spoke to Moses. Then the Jesuit contrasted that with Thomas Aquinas' definition. Finally he gave answers that came from the modern philosophers at the time of his writing, arising from their existentialist outlook.

What Murray did was to illustrate that even though we speak of God at different times and diverse places, the meaning of the name of God varied in different generations. Each era had given a different nuance, another perspective. Murray did not say that *God changes,* but rather that human perceptions of him do. Murray's words were very helpful to the priest who was still trying to match the God on the ceiling in his parish church with the experiences of God that he had discovered in his priesthood, in his pursuit of learning, but most of all in pastoral contacts, weekends and evenings in parish work. It was here particularly that he saw traces of God in the human beings and their meetings with him. As a priest he had been called to serve them, but he learned much more from them.

About that time, the Scripture revolution which had begun in the Catholic Church with Pope Pius XII's encyclical, *Divino Afflante Spiritu,* began to take hold. If you remember, that encyclical was the "Magna Carta" for Bible studies among Roman Catholic Scripture scholars. It allowed Catholics to understand that the books of the Bible came about in different ways and had varied audiences. The books exhibited a variety of literary styles, which expressed contrasting viewpoints even within the one Scripture. Central to this discovery for this priest were the insights provided by the careful and scrupulous scholarship of Sulpician Father Raymond Brown (particularly respected as the author of the Anchor series books on *The Gospel of St. John* and *The Epistles of St. John*). Father Brown's scholarship led the priest to read other estimable authors, each of whom helped him to discover the personality of Jesus Christ in a new and vivid way.

Like so many taught and raised in the Catholic schools in the 30's and the 40's, this author had always believed that Jesus the savior knew he was God from the very beginning. Yet the new Scripture scholarship opened his eyes to the fact that such a view did harm to the concept of Jesus as man. The new scriptural studies suggested that Jesus had to come gradually to his understanding of what God was asking of him. That view made Christ's response even greater. When the focus was on the faithful and loyal obedience of Christ to the will of the Father, it made possible a more appreciative understanding of the the role of Jesus as savior.

That kind of scholarship not only made this priest more aware of what we said when we ended every prayer, "Through Jesus Christ, Our Lord," but it also opened up a wonderful image of the Father. As he began to meditate upon the ways that Jesus himself discerned the Father, and the words He used to speak of the love of the Father, stressing his mercy and forgiveness, the stern image of the patriarchal figure on the ceiling of his parish church began slowly to fade from view. No longer was the Father the

"ancient of days" as William Blake had painted Him. No
longer was God "the timeless one." No longer was he seen
as stern and severe. Now the Father was seen through the
eyes of Jesus, and it was a revelation!

This was no little matter. While this author could sigh
for the fact that such Scripture scholarship was not
available earlier in his life, or that it had not even been
developed, the cleric was grateful to the Father of Jesus
who had revealed himself in such a way through study in
faith to those who wanted to learn more about him.

In the two decades since, many excellent books written
by Protestant scholars as well as Catholic, demonstrated
that the Gospels were written for specialized audiences and
different local churches. Along with others, he learned that
the Acts, that the Epistles themselves, were not all of a
piece. Yet for anyone who would be willing to search, there
were new discoveries helping to plumb the mysteries of
Jesus and his Father. To meet and speak of the Father of
Jesus—that gave a whole new dimension, a new definition of God, a new way to appreciate his patience with
this priest's weaknesses. It showed God's willingness to
forgive the faults and failings of this author who was striv-
ing, with many falls, to be a follower of Jesus, and to learn
with and through Christ what God was asking of him.

Somewhere in the course of his life, this author developed
a devotion to St. Teresa of Avila. He remembered one
biography of her, which described the difficulties that
remarkable woman had with churchmen, with her own
contemporaries, with some of her own Sisters. One story
remained with him in a particular way which revealed her

willingness to take on even God. It was said that while
Teresa was busy moving a convent from one place to
another because of necessity (in transporting people, furniture and food in carts, the move took place in the middle of a great thunderstorm), the carts got mired in the
mud up to the hubs. At that moment it was reported that
out of a flash of lightning, Teresa heard a voice say, "See
Teresa, see how I treat my friends?" To which it is reported
Teresa answered, "No wonder, God, you have so few."

Herein was another revelation. You could argue with
God. You could challenge him. You could question him.
You could ask why some things were happening. It demonstrated Teresa's intimacy with God, her friendly give
and take, and the exchange of good friends. The young
boy in this essay never could have debated with the God
the Father painted on the ceiling. But this "new" God, the
Father of Jesus, the one who loved and trusted his creatures
even though they failed him so much, was a God of whom
you could ask questions.

There are those who might think that because this writer
was a priest and was obviously working for God, programs
would go easier, that his work would naturally have God's
blessing, that because the priest's heart was usually in the
right place God was always going to guarantee success.
But the life of St. Teresa demonstrated that no, that was
not necessarily the case. As it turned out in reading other
kinds of books on spirituality, he discovered others, friends
of God, who were challenged by God, their friend in
heaven, who allowed things to take place which were never
planned, which harmed their work, set them back. Why,

God? For example, the program to do this and that and achieve so much good—why did it go awry and cause so much harm?

The priest remembered also from his philosophy studies the saying of the philosopher Etienne Gilson, who provided this insightful phrase, "Piety never dispenses with technique." That also put things in focus. It said that while it was fine to have a well-intentioned heart, if one did not know what he was about, if one did not develop skills or hone them to their best possible efficacy, piety would not save him from serious mistakes. Piety was never the way that would guarantee that something would work. Professionalism was the essence. That is why, as part of his search for God's face, the author has asked himself to continue interior growth, to keep learning, to revel in the new insights that were available as a result of the studies coming from Vatican II. The need was to become highly professional to do one's job well. It was an insight that in fact God was not always available to guarantee success for the well-intentioned if they had failed to live up to their basic responsibilities. It was also a reminder that the priest was obliged to do as much as he could always, while talking to God, sharing and letting God speak. That too was essential. Prayer was ever the ingredient that had to accompany the work, or it would suffer from the sin of pride.

That was a hard thing for any priest to learn. It was a hard lesson for this priest to appreciate. As his life moved on, those two points—the view of Teresa of Avila and the philosopher Gilson—came somehow to be part of his dealing with God. When circumstances took place that would ask him to change his life, he would ask God why, debate with God, argue that the plan God seemed to be proposing was not the best one. Yet because he had learned through the new insights into Scripture that Jesus had searched hard to find God's will, that in the middle of the way his life was going, he too asked hard questions, even of the Father. Yet in the end he had to submit humbly to the will of his Father. This had a great influence on the "me and God" and the relationship of the priest who became bishop almost against his will. That was one of the ways his life had to change, and he was not quite willing to have it go that way. In the end he, having learned of Christ, imitated his yes, but always kicking against the goad.

Surely one of Vatican II's emphases was on meeting God in the liturgy. That is one special way that is open always to the priest since he is usually an integral part of the liturgy. Does this priest who writes, meet God, for example, in the Mass? Yes, of course, but not to the extent that the liturgists would seem to want or indicate. After all, as "presider" (which is the current word for the old phrase, the "priest celebrant"), he is a public figure. His task is to gather together the vibrations and the intimations which come out of the people who are also celebrating the liturgy with him. He must be conscious of the public presence. There is no time for any private devotion during Mass (nor should there be, we suspect). There are those few moments when he is supposed to even lead in the silence, but leading in that silence is also a public act. So while he may strive to move into that silent section, which opens up the silence of God, the public liturgy is not the place for it.

Norbert F. Gaughan

How about "me and God" in the other sacraments? Oh yes, he could see the face of God sometimes in the married couples who came before him (if they were not too much influenced with the fads and goings on of what their wedding should be like to make it different). They can show how human love is—not merely an echo, but a great realization of the love of God for humanity. How about Baptisms? It was always a great joy to see the face of God in the new life which he has sent, or in the warmth and love of all who gathered around the baptismal font. In the old days, it was only the godparents who came. Now the family comes, which makes it a greater and richer moment, in which family pride, the reaffirmation of the human is perceived as all gaze upon the infant becoming part of the Church.

As bishop, this author also found the face of God in Confirmation, in the eagerness and anticipation of the young people to "be mature Catholics." Eagerness and anticipation, that is, if they have not been so psyched up by misguided Directors of Religious Education and others engaged in the kind of training which ended up making the sacrament an ordeal, similar to what the knights of old had to undergo before they could be knighted.

But as priest, and bishop, and sinner, he has found the face of God as mercy in the Sacrament of Reconciliation in the confessional. There happen those precious moments where you can almost hear God tiptoeing through the conscience of both priest and penitent (who are sometimes the one and the same), where great miracles had begun even before the penitent came into the confessional, or sometimes which happened after that extra help or understanding. In the Sacrament of Extreme Unction, the priest has gazed upon the face of God. He has discovered it amidst the anxiety and fearfulness of the family gathered around the sick bed, and in the attitude of the sick person particularly. Yes, there God as Mercy and Healer has shone through most brilliantly, which then reflected the trust of the human in God's goodness and generosity. Oh yes, liturgy can be a place where one can meet God as participant (as this person), or a sign of God's mercy in the priestly tasks.

How about liturgical prayer? Can one find God's presence there in what is now called the "Liturgy of the Hours"? Here, as a young boy, this author has been blessed. In his parish church, in that church where the stern visage of the patriarchal Father hovered over his childhood, he was fortunate to be an altar boy and to serve on a Sunday afternoon in what was called the Vespers. Every Sunday—that was the custom—the Latin words, mysterious, with great cadences, were sung by the congregation, and became part of the background against which he heard the praises of God proclaimed by ordinary folk. That public exercise of prayer became very special as the people sang the Sunday Psalms and it echoed the angelic choirs.

Now the priest-bishop says these Psalms in the English language, very often privately, sometimes in a hurry. They are a far cry from what was his experience as a boy. Yet, from time to time, a phrase, a verse of a Psalm, some line from one of the Church Fathers will jump out and demonstrate how even in olden days, God revealed himself to people who were searching for the face of God, to learn

Norbert F. Gaughan

his name, and to discover how they should relate to him, as they sang his praises.

In Brian Moore's 1987 novel, *The Color of Blood,* he created a character, a Cardinal of an Eastern European State similar to Poland. The Primate, Stephan Bem, caught up in the intricacies of trying to maintain the status quo between the government and the church, from time to time stops and tries not to debate with God but to create for himself a silence in which God would speak to him. (The question of silence has always been difficult for this American priest.) Brian Moore describes one of the Cardinal's prayer sessions: "As always, in prayer, in the act of prayer, he sought to open that inner door to the silence of God— God who waited, watched and judged." For this author, that "inner door to the silence of God" is a mood that still needs to be worked upon, still needs to become an easier practice. He's not quite certain about that business about "God who watched and judged." For that does not seem to be as he envisions the Father of Jesus.

Does not the watching and the judging become a little easier to accept because "me" has learned that this God is the Father of Jesus? That phrase has become a constant invitation to get to the Father through Jesus. Only then can "me" enter better in that silence of God, which will become more meaningful in the search to discover more about the personality of Jesus Christ. It's not easy. It's always a revelation that in this way, finding more about God, "me" can find out a great deal more about himself.

GOD, OUR HEAVENLY MOTHER

Kaye Ashe, O.P.

MY lifelong involvement with God began before I was conscious of it at that quiet moment of conception when the Spirit formed me in my mother's womb. It deepened on a winter's day some ten months later when my godparents bundled me off to the baptistery of Visitation Church and in my name renounced Satan and professed my belief in a God I had not yet experienced. No matter. God had taken hold of me and would not henceforth let me go.

Getting acquainted with God was dead easy for me, growing up as I did in an Irish Catholic family. Here God was something of a household word. He (for it would take me some time to think of God as other than male) was called upon often to help poor souls and to bless, love, or forgive this one or that. He always knew best and seemed frequently to agree with my parents. It was clear that he was a force not to be taken lightly, but he was more a familiar presence than a majestic being before whom we were to bow, scrape, and cower. Witness the reply of a neighbor when told one day that God's hand was in some particularly difficult situation. He exclaimed with evident feeling, "Well, I wish God would keep his hands in his pocket!" This God was everywhere: in the closet, under the table, in the teacups, on the porch, in the yard, behind

58

Kaye Ashe

the rising and setting of the sun. Like Janie in Zora Neale
Hurston's novel, we kept our eyes on God in good times
and bad and he kept his squarely on us.

Whereas at home God was an unseen but pervasive presence, from first grade on he became an object of study.
I learned multi-syllabic words to describe him, found out
that God was not one but three and yet mysteriously one,
and gradually came to know how to label those whose idea
of God and of Jesus, God-made-man, were sadly mistaken.
I grappled with notions of nature and person, concepts that
had daunted generations of theologians and had riven
Christendom but which were handily summarized for me
in the tidy questions and answers of the Baltimore Catechism. I looked with pity tinged with contempt on the few
Protestant kids in our neighborhood who not only were
not getting it straight about God but who had to go to
school on holy days of obligation. Furthermore, their
churches were pathetically devoid of statue and ornament.
The place where *I* encountered God was a neo-Gothic
splendor whose towers were visible for miles and whose
walls and windows were filled with reminders of the wisdom of Solomon, the sufferings of Jesus, the graciousness
of Mary, the courage of martyrs, the horrors of hell, and
the joys of heaven.

The Sinsinawa Dominican Sisters who furthered my education about God and his mysterious ways were short on
sentimentality and superstition and long on doctrine. There
was more emphasis on the Trinity than on the Sacred
Heart, and their favorite saints, Dominic, Thomas Aquinas, and Catherine of Siena, seemed to think a lot as well

59

as pray a lot and it was hard to imagine them in sappy poses or with the vacant eyes that sometimes stared out of holy cards.

Sister Virginia introduced me to the *Companion to the Summa* when I was a junior in high school, and I was immediately taken by the elegant arguments—arguments, for instance, that proved that God existed, for those who had any doubts about it. The familiar God of my youth, the God of Tuesday night novenas, the God whose crowned head and bloodied face I had contemplated with awe and fascination when I discovered it on my mother's *Tre Ore* booklet before I ever went to school, this God was now transformed for me into the Uncaused Cause, the Unmoved Mover, the Unchanged Changer, whose silence and immobility were nevertheless Pure Act. I wondered at my stupidity at having taken God for granted, because Thomas insisted that God's existence was *not* self-evident even if my parents seemed to think so. It was puzzling but somehow intensely pleasurable to read things like:

> God in himself is utterly intelligible, and does not have to wait for man to bring him to light as material objects do. But God as man sees him is not self-evident. There are reflections of God which are self-evident (thus the existence of truth, which is a reflection of God), but that there is a god existing separate from the bodily world with a nature of his own is not self-evident. The only things self-evident to us are things we know immediately by way of sense-experience; thus once we have seen wholes and parts, we know immediately and without any argument that wholes

are greater than parts. But to arrive at God from sense-experience, we must first recognize that what we see is caused, that this implies a cause, and that the ultimate cause transcends this bodily world. So we can arrive at God only by argument, and anything that must be argued is not self-evident.

This was tricky. Some elements of our experience like truth reflected God; that the element existed might be self-evident, but that it reflected God would require proof. I liked this probing, this making complex what was on the surface simple, this relentless examination of God's nature, God's perfection, goodness, eternity, oneness.

Dominican Fathers at Rosary College led me further through the limpid labyrinths of Aquinas' questions, definitions, and arguments. There was danger, I suppose, of the living God getting lost under the massive weight of syllogism, but then I would happen on a phrase in the *Summa* like "God is the most truly simple thing there is" and let that roll around in my head for awhile. Or, "One comes to God and one departs from him not by bodily movement, since he is everywhere, but by movement of the heart." Out from under the subtle distinctions shone a light which made it clear that for Aquinas, God was what we were seeking in our every desire and was at the heart of our every delight.

Perhaps it was the force of this truth that propelled me into the Sinsinawa Dominican novitiate. Propelled is far too strong a word, however, since I moved in with some reluctance and with a few long looks over my shoulder.

Nevertheless, I stayed and for two years God and I had a lot of time in which to get to know one another better.

Our novice mistress was loathe to let her impressionable charges loose on the mystics, but somehow I got my hands on the book *Showings* by fourteenth century English mystic Julian of Norwich. I was hooked. Thomas seemed to arrive at God through hard thinking and by way of philosophical argument. That had its attractions, but here was a woman whose knowledge of God was based on experience, on revelations, on "bodily visions" and "ghostly visions," that is, on imaginative visions and intellectual visions. The fact is both Thomas and Julian were at once theologians and contemplatives, but while Thomas wrote in the rational discourse of argument, objections, replies, and conclusions, Julian wrote in a charming, but far from facile, narrative. Her style is vivid, her language often that of courtly love. Her book has been characterized as "an artless masterpiece," and it intrigued me both in its expression and in its substance. My understanding of God and of God's closeness to all of creation broadened and deepened.

Julian's images made God so close, so good, so loving: "He is our clothing, who wraps and enfolds us for love, embraces us and shelters us, surrounds us for his love, which is so tender that he may never desert us." I marveled at the simplicity and the depth of passages like the following which I read and reread, savored, and pondered:

> God showed me something small, no bigger than a hazelnut, lying in the palm of my hand, as it seemed to me, and

it was round as a ball. I looked at it with the eye of my understanding and thought: What can this be? And I was answered, "It is everything that is." I was amazed that it could last, for I thought that because of its littleness it would suddenly have fallen into nothing. And I was answered in my understanding: It lasts and always will, because God loves it; and thus everything has being through the love of God.

It was Julian who taught me that God, neither Father nor Mother, can yet be imagined as both. She, however, seems more at home in describing the motherhood of God than the fatherhood, though in the end she achieves a synthesis that brought me to a better understanding of God and reflects, perhaps, her own psychological wholeness and spiritual integration. God, our heavenly Mother, is for Julian courteous, true, sweet, loving, precious, and wise. Her services are "nearest, readiest and surest." And, as J. Leclercq has demonstrated, Julian's reflections on God our Mother are not simply poetic musings. They constitute a theology of Trinitarian life. Later, thanks to feminist theologizing, I would see further theological, social, and political ramifications of introducing a feminine element into the Godhead. But more of that later. For the moment, the notion of God's motherliness simply enlarged my spiritual horizons and awakened me to new dimensions of divine beauty.

Julian, further, spoke to me of God's indwelling in accents I'd never heard before. If, even in my grade school days, I had been conscious of union with God ("you are the temple of the Holy Ghost"), my acquaintance with Julian illumined me exquisitely on this point. She writes:

> I saw no difference between God and our substance, but, as it were, all God; and still my understanding accepted that our substance is a creature in God. For the almighty truth of the Trinity is our Father, for he made us and keeps us in him. And the deep wisdom of the Trinity is our Mother, in whom we are enclosed. And the high goodness of the Trinity is our Lord, and in him we are enclosed and he in us.

And much more of the same until there was no escaping the truth that though separate, there was somehow nothing at all between God and my soul. This soul of mine, synonymous with divine goodness and grace, would forever love, thank, and praise God. Julian didn't exactly solve the problem of God's total transcendence and total immanence, because for her it was no problem. She was one with God, but God didn't, for all of that, swallow her up. Nor was God diffused and lost in creatures and creation. Julian helped me get the hang of seeing God as beyond all of creation and as yet yearning to be one with all of it. Her *Showings* stimulated my desire to be one with God.

The novitiate library shelves harbored another book that made a lasting impression on me and affected my image of God: *Pilgrim of the Absolute, Excerpts from the Writings of Leon Bloy*. Raissa Maritain made the selections and Jacques Maritain wrote the Introduction. Bloy was vehement and intuitive rather than rational, a fearful rather than a gracious visionary, and his writings riveted my attention. Here was a man who wept and raved in his pursuit of God; one who saw through the pretense, the shallowness, and often the cruelty of the bourgeoisie but who understood and loved the poor; one who had profound contempt for mediocrity, conventions, and conformity and who himself took account of nothing but God.

Voluntarily poor himself, Bloy revealed to me the God of the poor. Whatever the ambiguities of our vow of poverty, I was anxious to embrace it and thus dodge the awful imprecations that Bloy hurled at the unfeeling rich. "What must some day be so terrible an indictment of the rich," he wrote, "is the Desire of the poor."

> The rich do not expect the poor to have consolations or pleasures. The idea that some pauper might have bought himself tobacco or taken a cup of coffee is unbearable to them. They are right, without knowing it, since the poor are suffering in their behalf. But they keep their consolation for themselves, their appalling consolation, and what an agony they will undergo when, with each particle of their murderous riches demanding to be expiated by unspeakable atonements, they will see coming toward them that mountain of torments!

And the rich were not those whose coffers were full. No, anyone who possessed over and above what is indispensable to material and spiritual life, Bloy counted as a millionaire who was consequently a debtor to those who possess nothing.

GOD AND ME

Bloy's zeal for justice was an aspect of his love for God, and both were intense. Both informed his relentless quest for the Absolute, the only journey which for him had any meaning. Maritain characterizes Bloy as groping his way toward Pure Effulgence. Any other journey in which one imagines one is going somewhere is stupid, Bloy observed with his customary bluntness, and the faster one goes the more idiotic it is. But the pilgrim of the Absolute must not expect the journey to be a carefree quest. No, the pilgrim must move through deserts and must know cold, darkness, hunger, thirst, vast weariness, sadness, agony, and bloody sweat. Bloy scared me. His violence and prophetic wrath contrasted vividly with Aquinas' coolness and Julian's gracious optimism. But the fire in his heart enkindled one in mine, and through him I came to see another aspect of God's face.

During all of these years, Scripture, of course, provided a rendezvous with God. Here God revealed himself in the earthiness and naivete of some of the Old Testament figures, in the lyricism of the psalms, and in the untiring call of the prophets. And, of course, in Jesus—this Jesus who announced without fear the truth that his sensitivity and his love and his clear-sightedness uncovered; who revolutionized concepts of power, leadership, law, good, and evil; who so unerringly exemplified what was kind, loving, just, and godlike. God came alive in Mary's Magnificat and in the surprises and paradoxes of the parables. Some of the passages were over-familiar from years of repetition at Sunday Masses with homilies that lacked freshness and insight (to be as kind as possible about it), but the Dominican emphasis on Scripture urged me to explore books whose names I'd never heard of and to read familiar passages with new eyes. The passage in St. John, for instance, in which the wonderful repartee between Jesus and the Samaritan woman reveals so much about God's way with us.

My experience of God has been filtered, then, through family, parish, teachers, Scripture, and other writings. It remains to speak of nature, art, friends, and strangers.

There are those who in their hungering to know the principle that lies behind the mystery of their own lives and the life they see about them have settled on the sun, or trees, or the wind, and have worshipped them. And who can blame them? And who can deny that these things reflect the source of all life? There is a willow tree that I can see even now that speaks volumes to me of God's grace, of her fluidity, of her sorrow, and of her hospitality, for the willow welcomes all sorts of life and nourishes many creatures in her capacious bosom.

Nature's eternally changing and eternally remaining the same. Her exuberance, gaiety, mystery, and fecundity, her extraordinary generosity, indeed profligacy, her power, tenderness, vitality, and allure—all of this has provided me with glimpses of God and with excuses to speak with her or to remain in quiet awe or fascination before her terrible beauty. The Hebrews knew very well that God was to be found in nature. Elijah found him finally in a gentle breeze, but he knew the Lord was passing when he experienced the wind rending mountains and shattering rocks, when he felt the earthquake and saw flames of fire. And the psalmist awaited a God who would "come down like rain upon the mown grass: as showers that water the earth." God is rock and dew and mountain refuge in the Old Testament. He can be seen in fertile fields and heard from burning bushes.

If nature has revealed God's face to me, so have artists with their disconcerting way of seeing through and under things, juxtaposing the most unlikely things, arranging simple lines and colors into the most evocative compositions, clothing the most commonplace things in mystery, moving with such ease through the worlds of illusion and fantasy. It was especially when I came up against Romanesque, medieval, and Renaissance art in the churches and museums of Europe that I found God speaking out of stained glass windows, carvings, canvases, and frescoes. The Spirit was alive in these figures of the women and men of the Old and New Testaments, Mary, Jesus, the apostles, and saints. There was something here besides cunning craftsmanship, something beyond art for art's sake. The wonder, the longing, the sorrow or compassion, the simple love, the silent contemplation of these figures in glass, stone, wood, and oil spoke of the desire and faith of those who created them and of their conviction that the divine was tangible in the world around them. It would be difficult to look at them for very long without sharing that conviction. I could see now what people meant who called art God's deep mirror, a truth that had escaped me when my idea of a nice statue of Our Lady was a Hummel representation or one of those extremely slim, expressionless pieces popular in the '50s.

Kaye Ashe

And is God lurking in music and in literature? Yes, of course. And in theater. For all of these things have elements of play and of beauty; they are gratuitous but full of meaning. They remind us that God is lively and infinitely creative. Or is it only Bach, Michelangelo, Moliere, Charlotte Bronte, Twyla Tharp, and Leontyne Price who are lively and creative and ingenious? Should we sing our hymns to humanity instead of to the living God? Perhaps others are content to do so. Myself, I can't stifle the conviction expressed by Aquinas' treatise on the Divine Names: "The being of all things is derived from the divine beauty."

If my experience of God is ultimately intensely personal, this reflection on God and me makes me conscious of how intimately that experience is bound up with my cultural environment, and this has included elements as diverse as the Judeo-Christian tradition, Celtic Catholicism, the Western heritage with its Greek and Roman influences, and a little touch of American puritanism. These, together with the Dominican tradition, have provided me with a framework for imagining God; they have given me the means of interpreting my experience of the divine. Sometimes they've thrown up barriers to my attempt to understand God and myself, but generally they contain within themselves the correctives for their own limitations. I have no illusion that this combination of religious and cultural traditions has said the last word about God. I would like to know more about the African, Indian, and Oriental ways of speaking to and of God, aware that no single tradition has plumbed God's depth. I long ago outgrew my youthful complacency that having mastered the Catechism

I had definitively triumphed over Error and grasped Truth in its entirety.

And so I come to friends. What have they to do with God and me? A great deal because, as any neophyte in the ways of God knows, the best part of making any headway at all into God's inner life is experiencing a relationship of knowing and being known, loving and being loved. God's own inner life is essentially one of communication and loving relationship. We're called to share in it. But to share in it at all, I must have some experience of these realities somewhere this side of the Godhead. Indeed, it is the human-to-human experience of acceptance, trust, self-revelation, and mutual love that gives me some inkling of what goes on at the center of God's being and what can transpire between God and us. The love of friends, always unmerited and incapable of being commanded, makes me capable of believing in God's gratuitous love. The fact that they can see beyond my pettiness and jealousy and selfishness, indeed, can even coax me out of these things, lets me know I'm redeemable. If they are willing to make room for me, steal hours to spend with me, offer me the gift of their beauty and vulnerability and precious selves, rely on me not to betray their trust, and await these things from me, then I begin to get some idea of the kind of gift God offers and expects of me. Furthermore, friends intensify my pleasure in and deepen my knowledge about the other things that reveal God to me: nature, Scripture, literature, music, theater, art, fantasy, whimsy, and humor.

Strangers, too, intervene between God and me. Like

every child, I had been warned to beware of strangers. Strangers, foreigners, and aliens represent, after all, the unknown. Best be wary, then, if not downright hostile. But God, too, represents the unknown, and both God and the stranger challenge me to come closer, to do away with the wall that divides us. Scripture is clear about it: in welcoming the stranger, we welcome God. The stranger holds secrets about God that even friends cannot reveal to us.

God and I have gotten to know one another in more ways and through more means than I have commented upon here. But I would like to move on now to what has been a significant force in the last twenty years in bringing me to understand both God and myself better. This force is the feminist movement.

How has feminism affected my image of God? It reminds me that the way we image and speak of God in any age is the result not simply of personal prayer and spiritual musings; it is the result of social and political realities as well. Indeed, anything we say about God says more about us than it does about God. Theologians are aware of this when they remind us that we can really only say what God is not; no words of ours, no image will contain or reveal a God who is ineffable, incomprehensible, unimaginable, and inexpressible.

And so our image of God as a white, male patriarch is the faithful mirror not of God's reality but of a society dominated by white, older males. As that society begins to change, so do our images of God. As women and as people of color begin to think of themselves differently, they begin to think of God differently. Delivered from self-hatred, and seeing themselves as good and as sharing in the divine, they come to a new understanding of God. Images of God as male monarch and stern judge give way to images that bear a closer resemblance to themselves. The powerful words of the black woman and playwright Ntozake Shange give witness to this:

> i found God in myself
> and i loved her/i loved her fiercely.

These words conjure up a black, female God at the center of a black, contemporary woman. Whether they shock, excite, or inspire us, they force us to reexamine our notion of God.

While thinking of God as woman has become necessary and easy for many, and I include myself in their ranks, it continues to dismay others. A woman wrote to me recently that one of her difficulties with feminists was their habit of "making fun of God by addressing him in feminine pronouns (yuk)." That eloquent "yuk" expresses not only dismay but disgust. To suggest that God is female seemingly diminishes God. To clothe God in female garb is to ridicule God. God is, after all is said and done, Father, Son, Lord, and King. He is spirit, mind, reason, being, and pure act. He is intrinsically male. Woman is matter, body, instinct. She is weak and unworthy. She is all that God is not. The whole weight of biblical and Greek philosophical tradition and of theological pronouncements down the centuries militate against the notion of God as woman and woman as God.

Kaye Ashe

What then is behind the unholy urge of feminists to dislodge God the Father, to discredit images that have served us well, to disturb our notions of Trinity, to confuse our language and challenge our heritage? We can rephrase the question from another point of view. What moves us in the 20th century to rediscover God our Mother, to reconstruct theology, reinterpret biblical texts, reconceive history, and reimagine women's lives and meaning? Women's new sense of self and of female pride, women's reclaiming of our equality and intrinsic dignity move us in these directions. Women's new experience of strength, of worth, and power, sends us in search of a God in our image. And we have found her. We have tasted and savored the truth that women are made in God's image and share in the divine nature.

As women reclaim our divine inheritance, language, art, hymn, and symbol are beginning to reflect women's reality: women's creativity and fruitfulness, women's friendship, women's love of the earth and humanity, women's sacred history. In *The Mother's Songs, Images of God the Mother*, for instance, Meinrad Craighead, a former Benedictine Sister, flings out powerful images of a female God breathing life into creation and holding things together at the center. There is beauty, strength, and mystery in her images. They expand the horizons of our religious imagination.

It is not simply a question of creating something new, however. Reading Scripture with a feminist lens brings female images of God out of the shadows. We find notably Divine Wisdom personified as a woman, as one who is intelligent, holy, unique, manifold, subtle, agile, clear, spotless, kindly, tranquil, all powerful, the refulgence of eternal light, as one who herself unchanging, makes all things new. This is the God of whom Solomon says, "I determined to take her to live with me, knowing she would be my counselor while all was well, and my comfort in care and grief" (Wisdom 8:9). Association with her, he tells us, "involves no bitterness and living with her no grief, but rather joy and gladness." Wisdom, or Sophia, is sister, wife, mother, beloved, and teacher.

This imaging of God as woman makes it easier for women to think of themselves as worthy and to relate to God as to an intimate friend. In a recent conversation among women, several such images emerged. Judy Vaughn of the National Association of Women Religious spoke of working with minority women whose relation with God was heavily conditioned by their relation with men in whom they often found oppressors. They tended to look upon God as policeman and judge from whom they could expect sentence and punishment. Judy decided to hang a picture of a benevolent old Bolivian woman in her office. When women asked who this was, Judy would reply that it was her image of God. The women receiving this news relaxed, smiled, and obviously relished the idea of God in the guise of a warm, kind, dark woman much like themselves.

Patty Caraher, a Dominican Sister, spoke of God as an old woman with white, flowing hair and a voluminous and vividly red gown reaching to her bare toes. This woman appeared to her one day, emerging from a tree and approaching her as she sat on a sandy shore. The woman invited Patty to walk along the shore with her, and Patty remarked on her grace and lightness. Finally, the old woman stepped into the water and beckoning Patty to come forward she took her into her arms, lifted her, and then rocked with mighty laughter that shook her from head to toe. Patty said to herself, "This is God!" and since that moment feels most entirely and freely herself when she remains close to the woman God in red.

Images such as these: female images of God as Wisdom, as Bolivian peasant woman, as a light and laughing old woman in red, free, expand, and enrich my ways of thinking about God. But it is not just a question of God and me. Our images of God go beyond the personal realm; they reflect and influence the world about us. If we believe in male and female equality, if we believe both are made in God's image, then it is essential to think and speak of God as both female and male. God is inadequately represented by any image, but the exclusive use of male images can no longer be justified. We must see God as mystery, sovereignty, strength, beauty, power, and love—and look upon both men and women as equally able to represent all of that. When we recognize that each person of the Trinity transcends categories of male and female but can be legitimately imagined as either, then we can begin to foster male-female relations marked by equality and reciprocity. Our image of God as male and female can pave the way for a true community of women and men, one in which mutuality replaces privilege and subjection. If we achieve this at the very basic level of gender, it becomes easier to let fall the barriers of race and class, the other categories with hierarchical arrangements of superior and inferior.

Women are not alone in looking beyond God the Father. Thirty years ago Alan Watts observed in *Beyond the Spirit*, "Since we are men, we shall always be to some extent compelled to talk, think, and feel about God in our own image." (It is interesting to note that like so many authors, he addresses himself to a male audience.) He invited men, however, to look beyond a purely male God and to discover God as playful, supple, graceful, exuberant, as beautiful and alluring. He encouraged them, that is, to seek the feminine face of God. Indeed, he declared the male God dead because such a God is rigid, solemn, stiff, fixed, tense, and righteous.

I am aware of the perils in this line of thought. We risk perpetuating stereotypes when we associate power, authority, and strength with men; grace, fluidity, compassion, and beauty with women. There is danger of entrapping men and women in their roles and in so doing to exclude women from the exercise of leadership and men from the realm of nurturing love. I offer Watts, nevertheless, as representative of men who are acutely conscious of the limits and the inadequacy of imaging God solely as man, father, Lord, and King.

Women theologians have since gone far beyond Watts in examining our images of God and bringing to light what they tell of ourselves. For, in the end, Watts presents us with a God of robust masculinity, "the embodiment of *true* manliness. . .because his nature contains a subordinate feminine element." Women thinkers and women pray-ers,

Kaye Ashe

invite us rather to imagine the unimaginable, incomprehensible God in terms that avoid male idolatry, gender division, and gender stereotyping. It is not simply a question of imagining the stubbornly male God as now rather more attractive because more tender, merciful, and loving, in short, more like a woman. It is not even a question of granting womanhood, let us say, to the third person of the Blessed Trinity. It is rather a question of becoming capable of imaging God *equally* as male or female. We need not reject, abandon, or kill God the Father properly understood. But we must be able, too, to represent God simply as woman or as God the Mother and see or hear her represented so with joy rather than with indignation or dismay.

I discovered an image recently that speaks to me of God. It is a woodcut by Sister Chiara Pauloni entitled "She Stoops to Us." It pictures a limber feminine figure bent in an arc, her arms and her entire body enveloping and protecting a small child. She doesn't, however, impede the child's freedom of movement. She listens to the child, who whispers confidently into her ear. The woman's dress seems made of leaves; her hair falls in streams that finally pierce the ground and appear to root her to the earth. Here I find a reminder of the divine reality whom I shall continue to seek in wind, sea, sky; in works of art; in Scripture; in father, brother, sister, and mother; in friend and stranger; in the eyes of the poor and the outcast; and at my own center. And I shall love her fiercely wherever I catch a glimpse of her because I shall recognize in her the source of all that is good.

GOD AND ME

I conclude with a prayer inspired by Sister Chiara's woodcut and by Julian of Norwich's *Showings:*

All loving, all good, all beautiful God,
    in whom we are endlessly born
    and from whom we shall never part,
You encompass all that is.

You stoop to us.
You envelop, embrace, and welcome us.
You are the Goodness that kindles our soul
    and brings it to life.

We seek you, and shall ever seek you
    until we know truly
    that we are all enclosed
    within you.

In your presence we reverently wonder
    and are often surprised.
Your endless life living within us
    makes us peaceful and at ease,
    harmonious and flexible.
In you we have space, life and being.
Amen.

"...THE THINGS OF A CHILD"

Edwin Chase

I MUST admit that I have always been envious of those few people I've actually known, and those many others who have written devotional, mystical and spiritual books, who claim to have a personal relationship with Mary, with Jesus, with God.

They refer almost casually to encounters, promptings, even dialogue with Our Lady, Our Lord, Our Father. This intimacy is not given to everyone, of course, but it is implicit as a goal of the spiritual life in classic Catholic writings, exercises, and "ways." One cannot expect to hear the voice of the divine, or to attain the precious unity without following a difficult, structured and often frustrating regimen of meditation and prescription by a spiritual professional or advisor. This sort of high altitude mysticism was always rare, and nowadays seems pretty much extinct.

But according to sociologists, many people still have fairly frequent mystical experiences of varying degrees of intensity. And they have them more or less out of the blue. That is, they happen outside any formal spiritual regimen and even when the subjects are not actively seeking them. These are rarely verbal in nature but there is always a sense of transcendence and union with something or someone far more expansive than the subject's normal limits of awareness of self-perception.

GOD AND ME

More common yet are the experiences of those who report that in times of prayer or meditation, they hear an inner voice, distinctly not their own, which offers direction, counsel, consolation and which, in time, they come to personify as that of Jesus or the Holy Spirit.

As noted, I am envious of these people because I have never had such a close encounter. Once, in the third or fourth grade of a parochial school, early in the morning before having anything to eat, I went to take up my assigned vigil in church for Forty Hours Devotion. After kneeling erect on the unpadded oak prie-dieu for twenty or thirty minutes, eyes glued to the seductive golden rays of the monstrance, I sensed some movement, a rustling flutter off to the side. A statue of Mary, as familiar as the back of my hand, stood there. Had she smiled and opened her demurely clasped hands toward me in that glimmering moment? My heart pounded. My eyes rolled. I fainted dead away. But I did that rather often in those days. "Church sickness" was endemic amongst youngsters made to kneel fasting in crowded, poorly ventilated pews each school-day morning.

I think I was devout. I certainly believed literally all that I was told and taught. Jesus, his Sacred Heart pulsating over his spotless white and flowing, seamless robe, walked the holy card roads of someplace called Galilee. Mary exuded maternal vigilance and love, moving from her pedestal only when she stood sorrowing beneath the cross in the bas-relief of the Stations grown grimey on the walls above the side aisles. God the Father was a fierce, disembodied eye who resided in a triangle carved on the fron-

80

tispiece of the pulpit. In the round window above the main altar, the Holy Ghost, a superior pigeon, bombed hapless, earthbound apostles with red tongues of fire.

But even when I had grasped and believed the fullness of the meaning of the symbols, none of them ever sought me out or spoke to me. Not that I didn't talk to them in the stylized language of the missals and pamphlets that I thumbed. (Oh the difference, the ego-oiling status of owning an imitation Morrocco bound Father Steadman's Missal rather than the standard issue black paper version with no marker ribbon!): "Lord grant me this. . . ." "Remember, Oh most gracious Virgin Mary, that I want. . . ." "For these and all the sins of my past life, I am most heartily sorry." "Oh Lord I am not worthy. . . ."

Confession—first Confession—frightened me. I never liked the dark box. I hated it. But if the nuns taught me anything, it was the terrible reality of sin—not evil, but my personal guilt in the eye of that Triangle God on the pulpit, who was just barely able to restrain himself from casting me into the fires of hell. This conviction took a quantum leap with the onset of puberty when such venial sins as disobedience and lying gave way to the mortal graveness of any and everything associated with (let's not play with such euphemisms as sexual curiosity or natural attraction) lust. Keeping my slate clean of "impure thoughts, glances, and actions" was a full-time vocation. I remember riding my bike to Saturday afternoon confessions with exaggerated caution lest I be killed en route and hurled into the abyss. It was perfectly clear to me that the fact that I was making the effort to get to the box would count for nothing to the Eye. The path to hell is paved with just such foolish assumptions.

I found the act of confessing debasing and abhorant. But I went. Much later, as a student at a Catholic university I fell into true psychological scrupulosity and became convinced that everything I was doing was probably sinful, and that I was doomed further by hardness of heart. I went to confession twelve times in a single month, never to the same priest twice. Finally, unwittingly, I did a repeat of my neurotic little act.

"You were in here with this stuff last Tuesday, weren't you?" asked the priest (Blessed be his name!). "I want you to do us both a favor. Get out of here now and don't come back to me or any other confessor for a month. I don't care if you steal the pope's ring or have sexy thoughts about a sultan's whole harem. You've got my pass for a month. Forget about sin; get on with your life, man!"

It's been about fifteen years, now, since my last Confession. I went into a Franciscan church in the heart of a large city and rattled off a fairly prosaic list of minor transgressions. This was answered by almost a full minute of silence, followed by an enormous sigh.

"Truly tragic," said a guttural voice.

"I think your problems run deep and must be countered by radical attention to personal hygiene. With many women the fear of sexual arousal makes them avoid the proper ablutions of the private organs...."

Now I'm no Sly Stallone ("Yo, God have I sinned!") but I don't have a high piping voice. "Father," I tried to rumble, "I'm a man."

Edwin Chase

"Don't interrupt," the priest told me (though I often wondered if it was truly a priest behind the grill or some dingbat who had wandered in off the city sidewalks to hide out in the box). "The secret lies in proper douching...."

I got up off my knees, opened the door and nearly ran out of the church. The experience made something click in my head. I had evidently gotten off on the wrong foot with the whole business of confession and things were never going to get better. I decided that God must know all my sins by now and I was never any the better for recounting them to a priest. Forgiveness was God's to give or withhold as he pleased. I have never suffered a moment's twinge of regret or nostalgia for the hostile confines, even though I know I have a false, shallow and wrong-headed appreciation of a Sacrament rich with meaning and grace for others.

At first, I did much better with the Eucharist. The nuns rehearsed us for First Holy Communion for weeks. The big day came, complete with white suits and frilly white frocks. I think I was not alone in being so concerned with following rehearsal routine to the letter ("Walk, don't skip.... Genuflect all the way down.... Turn left exactly on the white mark.... Open your mouth wide and stick out your tongue, but don't drool and whatever you do, if the host sticks to the roof of your mouth, don't try to pick it off with your fingers....") that I blocked out any real reaction to what we were led to expect would be a monumental experience. I did whisper the proper devotional formulae to myself and welcomed Jesus to my heart, even though it was pretty obvious that he was headed for my stomach. I wondered if he stayed only until he dissolved

GOD AND ME

or would he work his digested way into my bloodstream and get into my heart that way?

These technical questions were soon forgotten in the flurry of photographs and rich outpouring of parental and avuncular pride. We were give a magnificently ornate scroll and allowed to keep our personal processional candles, made of pure beeswax and embossed with insets of gold and red paschal lambs. I hoped Jesus was well clear of the pancakes and bacon I gorged on an hour later at the family cafe.

Here again, I must somehow have gotten off to a bad start. I tried very hard to make the leap of faith or mind or whatever it is that most good Catholics evidently soar through with ease. That consecrated host is the body and blood of Jesus for them each and every time they receive. Whereas for me, it was only with the utmost effort of will that I could make that leap and, having made it, I would immediately slide back down into that faithless pit in which bread and wine—those deceptive "accidents" of real appearance, won the day.

Perhaps that's why I never heard the close, small voice in my heart or head. Somehow it really didn't make much difference whether the Eucharist was "Do this in memory of me," or actually the physical "me" of Jesus. Invisible daily miracles of that magnitude just didn't seem likely to a kid who had just delivered the morning paper. If they were, I should have been transformed, the world should dim and fade away.

I kept going to Communion of course, and berating myself for my shameful doubts (which I confessed). Through

84

all my formative years I had no question that everything the Church taught, and every word of Scripture I chanced upon was absolutely and literally true. The problem must lie with me and my ignorance and hardheadedness. Why? Because so many good people, and not just good, but intelligent, educated, well-read people believed it and evidently lived it.

Adolescence is a necessary but troubled time. In the process of searching for a personal identity distinct from the familial tribe, the young person begins to discern contradictions between what adults—even parents—say and what they do. The amount of tacit hypocrisy on which the world turns is staggering. Mentors, role models, whole codes, systems and institutions have cracks in their pedestals which quickly tumble them into the dust of teenage scorn. There is little balance, tolerance, or compassion in these sudden judgments. One corrupt or heavy-handed policeman makes all "cops" pigs. "You smoke (drink, swear, skip work), why can't I?" And so it goes.

I was certainly not exempt from this process. But I was particularly alert to any and every form of religious shortcoming. This had two consequences—one negative and one far more important positive result.

On the down side, I approached every new exercise in religious education with mounting scepticism. In Catholic high school I took to playing the role of the Devil's Advocate, pointing out every contradiction and weak spot I could discover. On the one hand the Brothers who taught us were delighted with what seemed to be my special interest and attention in religion courses which most of my fellow students suffered through with barely disguised indifference. On the other, my constant challenges sometimes posed difficulties and even disruption when, after some lengthy explanation made for my personal enlightenment, I would insist that it was simply saying the same thing in another way and failed to meet the issue.

In retrospect, I can hardly blame them. They were used to deference and quite sure that the stock answers of their apologetics background were iron clad and bound to carry the day—especially against mere striplings. I passed all the courses but was ejected from more than one class, and told to stay away until I could muster more respect and a better attitude.

I won't belabor you with the specifics of these arguments; they were fairly banal and far from original. It did seem to me that what we had been taught as the literal truth of revelation as children was now being qualified, softened, sometimes even withdrawn in an attempt to make it both palatable to the adult mind and more defensible to the onslaughts of other philosophies, as well as compatible with the empirical truths of science. And in the process throwing Baby Jesus out with the bathwater of what really didn't hold up.

This mind-set went with me to college, through tortuous hours reading Aquinas and scriptural exegesis. Somehow the more I learned the more sceptical I became. I think I am one of those perverse Catholics who would have been better off without the (in my case rather extensive) benefits of "adult education." I still have many grave problems, especially with the age-old conundrum of suffering and evil. But it finally dawned on me that most of these diffi-culties of mine were with fairly petty specifics of religious claims, issues, practice and moral authoritarianism which, when put into the larger perspective of the questions of the nature of the reality of God and humankind's place and destiny in the universe, really amount to very little.

It also is becoming clearer that my steadily mounting aversion to formal worship and religious ritual—my adult version of "church sickness"—should not be allowed to let me slip into a sort of agnosticism of indifference. If I didn't spend as much time in churches, on my knees (because I only grow angry at the music, the constant singing, the by now totally familiar readings, and the all-too-often hor-rendous homilies), I had better make some quiet times of my own, had better "pray" in some meaningful fashion. It's easy to knock the system, but it's not always easy to replace it effectively.

The positive side of my critical approach to all things religious emerged slowly over the years. Even as I found what I thought were too many man-made (all right, per-son-made) accretions and accommodations inherent in what we were taught was strictly divine doctrine, I seldom found personal hypocrisy in the priests and religious who did the teaching and the preaching, the ministering, the caring for the sick and the aged—or in any of the hun-dreds of other good religious people I have known. Almost without exception these Christians lived out their convic-tions. They did things for other people for the sake of do-ing good; they cared for caring's sake.

If I couldn't experience or communicate with God direct-

GOD AND ME

ly, and only very dimly and very seldom through religious rite and practice, it was possible to feel his existence and presence vicariously in the impact he made on the lives of others.

Further reflection along these lines finally helped me to come to at least partial terms with the problem of suffering, death, and the evil which humankind inflicts upon each other—even the seemingly contradictive and casual evil with which nature, disease and famine seem to mock the notion of a God who is so caring and benign that he watches "the sparrow" fall. One simply has to accept the fact that God doesn't normally interfere or intervene in the laws and forces, the random catastrophes of nature. Nature is "red in tooth and claw." Ten thousand mayflies perish against the mantle of my kerosene lamp. The food chain is a conveyor belt in a slaughterhouse.

It is sheer illusion to believe that humanity is somehow privileged or exempt from these harsh realities. Millions died in the holocaust. A hundred thousand are swept away by a tidal wave. An Ethiopian baby dies at its mother's withered breast. Cancer is promiscuous in choosing its victims. School buses fall off cliffs. Only the good die young. God's in his heaven but not all's right with a world where people kill each other daily in his name.

But I came to see, finally, that because God permits these things to happen doesn't mean that he wants them to happen. Mysterious are his ways, to be sure. But if the Lord taketh away, he also giveth. Life, all life, nature, all nature, has origin in him and is sustained by him in a fashion of his own immutable devising. It is not a plan that

88

we can fully fathom. About all we can say for sure, with Pierre Teilhard de Chardin, is "something is afoot in the universe."

So God doesn't go about making all things right in the best of all possible worlds. He has given us all existence, life, and demonstrated his love—for Christians in a special way through the incarnation of that love. If we receive it without reservation, as it is given without reservation, then we become an extension of that love. It is through good and loving people that God intervenes against and mitigates all evils. Jean Paul Sartre said that "hell is other people." He was wrong, God is other people.

He is there in the anguished eyes of the starving Ethiopian mother and in those of the jubilant mother who has just given birth to a healthy baby in a modern urban maternity center. He was there in the helping hands on the deck of the sinking Titanic. He is there in the passion of lovemaking. He can be heard in a symphony by Mozart. He can be felt in the morning breeze off a lake. Truly, he is everywhere.

I have had a curiously trouble-free and happy life (my turn will come, I know) but in my long winter of hardheartedness, I resisted crediting such fullness and happiness to a God who could wreak such wanton affliction on others. I certainly didn't deserve it, or earn it; in fact, if there were any justice, such blessings should fall into the lives of others who followed all the rules and devoted their lives to others.

I reached the conclusions outlined above—finally—on my own. But I came across something written by Daniel

Pilarczyk, Archbishop of Cincinnati, which sums it up better than I have been able to do:

"When it comes to accepting the offer of God's love for us, these reasons for holding back are simply absurd. When God extends his arms to us and says, 'Come and live with me,' our reasons for hesitating just don't make any sense. 'I can't afford what it costs.' Of course we can't afford what it costs, because it's not for sale. 'I don't want anything I haven't worked for.' In that case, we might as well just stop living right now, because our very life and everything we have in life is already God's gift. 'I don't deserve it.' Obviously we don't deserve it. God doesn't expect us to. In fact, the one thing God asks from us is to admit that we don't deserve his gifts, and then to accept them anyway. God is bigger than our human hangups and failures and sins, and to try to make God subject to the same dynamics that we use in our ordinary life is to try to cut him down to our human size. *It is to love darkness rather than light.*"

CREDO

Martha Vertreace

AS I wrote "Credo," I listened to various contemporary voices—to John Shea's playful obsession with locating the sacred in the commonalities of human life, to Thomas Merton's mysticism, emergent from his involvement in world concerns. Most of all, I listened to the voice of Scripture, especially as I let my imagination take me along the road to Emmaus, a personal journey in faith. I tried to experience myself along such a road with friends, encountering a Stranger who would break open the past for us in such a way that our lives would become more creation-centered, more celebrative. What memories would we cherish and ritualize in artistic expression with our twentieth-century hindsight?

Credo

Evening fell as grey mist in the lindens.
For years, shadows inched overland,
crept through locked doors, shuttered windows.
At crossroads, we listened
for his footsteps as night choked every voice,
save the dense trembling of leaves
tumblin' under winter weight
like kamikazi warriors.

Clouds blew out stars one after one.
The lake lay still-born, green as ever

GOD AND ME

we'd seen it, and just as cold.
No familiar signs remained.
The road stretched far ahead.

What do we remember in this frozen land?

We had favored crystal, a brackish taste,
as blood thinned to seawater. We struggled
for a glimpse of our past smothered
in flames and ash. When our eyes
stung with mineral wash, our feet sank,
salt pillars in the Cities of the Plains.

Then his words reached us—called us
from Lazarus' tomb to the birthing cave.
Stumbling over grave wrappings,
we ran to greet him, death oils
dripping from every gasping pore
crusting in the sun
which seared our eyes awake.

We ate the dust of our shame
as rocks cast blaming shadows.
But he touched sand into graphic silence
and when no one spoke, we sat laughing
at mourners, turning from death chants and flutes.

Through mountains-plains-forests
deserts-oases, we tagged along.
Hungry and thirsty, he shared with us
the little that he had and we all shared
until four five thousand million ate

Martha Vertreace

fish and corn bread and gumbo
polish sausage and tortillas and paella
subgum pork and pemmican.
We filled several doggie bags
with left-overs.

We remember double-digit inflation
devalued dollars
quarter sandwiches with copper filling
a graduated income tax that flunked
the poor woman who dropped pence
in the alms box and they laughed
and laughed when they told him
to pay pew rent
but he burned bingo boards
and set fire to chances on the red Porsche
shredded tickets to baseball games
and Las Vegas Night.
The last laugh was ours
when we gave Caesar silver dollars
from the mouth of the Fish.

We found the north star
sleeping in the lap
of the crescent moon.

What were his words—what do we remember—
     I will make you fishers of men
     of women of children
     of those who cradle in their mothers' wombs
     and those who sleep in death's unquiet bed.
We cast our nets into the night sky
and drew in a myriad of stars.

GOD AND ME

He loved the beautiful woman
      sand-colored woman
      long-haired woman
round like a harvest moon
skin cool as nard
smooth as the alabaster jar she broke
to grieve his death
to celebrate her rebirth.
He loved the others too—
busy Martha attentive Mary
followers of Joanna and Susanna
daughter of Jairus
woman who touched his cloak
widow of Naim
woman of Samaria
Mary his mother
and all the others
Joan of Arc
Clare of Assisi
Emily Dickinson
Amelia Earhart
Susan B. Anthony
Winnie Mandela
Sacajawea
Rosa Parks
Nancy and Emerine Miller
Modena and Marie Kendrick
Peggy Scott
Bess Morrissey
and all the others
but best of all and all
he loved the beautiful woman

Martha Vertreace

      sand-colored woman
      long-haired woman
whose tears troubled the waters
of Bethesda.

We crouched low in the hull
tossed between storm and surge
frothing over the side.
Darkness strained against our oars.
He came to us, his steps unbroken,
      olive oil on water.
Dying in our fear,
rising to the touch of his hand,
we yearned to reach him
as doubt imprisoned us
in a whirlpool.

Head pillowed, he slept, although
no dry spot remained. We woke him
begging for our very lives.
      Seas lay stilled,
      winds becalmed.
Then we knew
our minds were yet too small;
we had not understood.

Kids—we remember kids—
who sat on his lap
pulled his beard
teased him, fed him,
listened to his stories
in round-eyed wonder.

GOD AND ME

How could we become like them?
We build the kingdom stone on stone,
but can we re-enter our mothers' wombs,
and can they again lie a-birthing?

The stones would cry out
had we stood mute.
We jumped up and down
cheering as when the Bears
won the Super Bowl.
Palms lent their fronds
and we our coats to pave the way.
The stones would not be outdone:
>agate turquoise sapphire
>carnelian beryl jasper
>onyx quartz chalcedony
>topaz amethyst diamond.

Refusing to become bread
which today is eaten but tomorrow molds,
stones became the cornerstone
but the road led to a Trail of Tears,
the Middle Passage, Auschwitz.

Remember all the stories he told
around campfires ablaze with cedar,
perch crackling over knotty pine—
not rabbinical midrash
not the latest exegesis
just stories of home
>woman finding a coin
>woman kneading leaven into meal

Martha Vertreace

          wedding feast
          forgiving father
just stories of work
          farmer who sowed seed
             all over the place
          field sown with weeds and wheat
          son in the vineyard with the vintner's tenants
          shepherd's search for one lost sheep
just stories of creation
          barren fig tree
          mustard seed.

Himself the Word made flesh
told living stories
all the ancient secrets
which lay hidden
since before the beginning
          and sometimes he would say
             did you get it
          and sometimes we would say
             no we didn't.

THE HIND PARTS OF GOD

Martin E. Marty

FATHER HENRI NOUWEN sat across the table. He ruined my dinner. As reliable a spiritual guide as one could want, he casually opened a conversation that disturbed my peace. "Isn't it about time you took a long and profound spiritual retreat?" Nouwen would arrange a Jesuit version of one, based on Loyola's *Spiritual Exercises*, if I would give a month for the experience at Guelph, Ontario.

Why retreat? Because, said Nouwen, he had discerned that when I wrote on spiritual subjects I tended—the term was mine—to "hitch-hike" on the accounts of experience by religious geniuses, who inspired my search and response. "It is time, isn't it, for you to find out what is in you? To experience God directly, as it were?"

Nouwen described the discipline of seeking in ever richer detail. At first his combined nudge and offer sounded attractive. A month away from telephones, airports, ordinary duties: who could ask for more? Even the disciplines he described of waking up in the middle of the night at the direction of a spiritual director were not jarring to someone given over to the Protestant ethic.

The price kept getting higher as Nouwen spoke, however, and I began to break into a coolish sweat. "You would pray for three hours at times, meditate for three hours at others." It is hard for me to sustain three minutes of solitary prayer before the mind wanders, and efforts at meditation usually lead me to drop off in slumber. "And, of course, no books. No books. Only the Bible, as your director opens it for your contemplation. You are to focus on God."

Now the sweat poured, my hand holding tableware trembled. Ask me to take on the Seattle Seahawks' defensive line, enter the Olympics, direct Mahler's Eighth, sky dive, try to scale Everest—none of these would induce more panic than the idea of that bookless month of contemplation, of attempting directly to experience God.

Dessert came, the topic changed, I recovered. Of course, I never took the retreat. In the light of dawn, perspective began to come. Personally, theologically, esthetically, existentially: it occurred to me that I did not crave the experience Nouwen was describing. Maybe I should have, but I did not and do not. The approach ran against all I was trained to look for or be content with; its risks differed from the risks I was schooled to undertake.

Put most simply, traditional contemplation of the sort that Nouwen was portraying (or at least that I was hearing or translating—these paragraphs may not do justice to his nuances) hinted at a kind of "union with God at God's level," as it were. And all my instincts are to crave a condescending God, a self-emptying God, a meeting with God at the human, even the most intensely human level.

Discerning readers, who may be at the point of wearying of the "I" or the "me" assigned each of us by the editor, might now or soon begin to sense where this is going. Catholic contemplative Nouwen and I, the Lutheran across the table from him at Cambridge one night, no doubt share—clear the throat and tongue!—Athanasian Trinitarian Chalcedonian Christological orthodoxy about God. Neither of us may be able to penetrate all that the creed-makers meant by the Greek words they used to describe God. We may have to be content with some translation, some puzzlement, some contentment with the *intention* of the framers of creeds, as we understand those intentions, rather than with all the hard-to-grasp words. Yet we would still share orthodoxy.

However, asked to say how things are between "God and Me," as this book title has it, Nouwen and I would no doubt begin to part company when it comes to the issue of how God is chiefly experienced, what one witnesses to in speaking of contact with God. (Needless to say, I do not speak for Nouwen, or Catholic contemplatives or philosophers, but am setting up an alternative as an "ideal type" to contrast the piety and theology that shape me and my kind.) Once again, the discerning will spot from everything that follows that the coming together of "God and me" is prismed through a version of interpretations cherished by Lutherans and other Christians like them.

That observation may sound as dull and boring as the Catholic orthodoxy we share sounds to the anti-dogmatic. But neither orthodoxy nor Lutheran piety and theology need turn out to be bland or settled. Should one apologize for not being able to escape one's upbringing? Nurtured by parents who taught and lived and believed well, by pastors who articulated what spoke clearly to the soul, teachers who now and then and eventually most of the time

Martin E. Marty

transcended the deadness and legalism that afflicts Lutheranism gone bad, books that frightened and exhilarated—I have had thousands of reasons to test the upbringing.

Either lacking the imagination or the desire to escape this matrix, I have chosen to let it stun me at times and cause me to soar at others. Lutheran God-talk, after all, has been the main impetus for everything from modern "death of God" talk—all those Nietzscheans were brought up Lutheranly—to numbing, sterile, crabby, and cramping sectarianisms (with some wonderful stops along the way). One last "needless to say," there is no interest here in being either sectarian about Lutheranism or cultic about Luther; one chafes at the thought of either. Keep thinking instead of a prism, a basis for grasp, a perspective, a way of saying a first word.

At best, such an approach allows people of other Christian (or religious) traditions who do some comparing a chance to be aware of, entertain, and perhaps adopt some views of God that complement or jostle their own. At worst, it allows readers to learn of a primal Lutheran accent that, I fear, rarely comes through in Lutheranism. In 1983, the year of Martin Luther's 500th anniversary, an interviewer put it shockingly and thus well: "Why is Luther so interesting, and why are you Lutherans so damn dull?" There is no damndullness in Luther's own approach.

Here is the heart of it all, the exchange that leads me to make the theme of my witness the "hind parts," the "back side," the "posterior" or, were I not risking being misunderstood, the "buttocks" of God as the primal and sustaining experience. It all goes back to a formal dispute

101

GOD AND ME

Martin Luther engaged in at a meeting of the (and his) Augustinian Order at the University of Heidelberg on April 26, 1518. There in Theses 19 and 20 we read in words none of which (well, one, 'man' = 'person') would I change:

"19. The man who looks upon the invisible things of God as they are perceived in created things does not deserve to be called a theologian."

20. The man who perceives the visible rearward parts of God as seen in suffering and the cross does, however, deserve to be a theologian."[1]

> [1]The Latin reads: *"Non ille dignus theologus dicitur, qui invisibilia Dei per ea, quae facta sunt, intellecta conspicit. Sed qui visibilia et posteriora Dei per passiones et crucem conspecta intelligit."* The best, though badly translated, work on this subject is Walther [ed: yes, Walther, not Walter] von Loewenich, *Luther's Theology of the Cross* (Minneapolis: Augsburg, 1976); I have also depended upon Alistair E. McGrath, *Luther's Theology of the Cross* (Oxford: Blackwell, 1985), Chapter 5, especially at one or two crucial points.

In these theses the antagonist was a view of God against which Luther was reacting and which he may have been partly stereotyping, just as I may well have caricatured the invitation to contemplation and Catholic piety tendered me at the dinner table across from Henri Nouwen.

The reference here is to Exodus 33:23. Moses, on Sinai, wants to undertake a spiritual retreat, to contemplate God, to aspire to a vision "head on," as it were. The Jerusalem Bible has Moses say: "Please show me your glory." The

Lord instead revealed the name "Yahweh," and announced grace and pity. "But my face you cannot see, for no human being can see me and survive." Then Yahweh said, "Here is a place near me. You will stand on the rock, and when my glory passes by, I shall put you in a cleft of the rock and shield you with my hand until I have gone past. Then I shall take my hand away and you will see my back; but my face will not be seen."

The use of this passage by Luther and those in his tradition is typically outrageous and thus potentially creative and faithful; so it must be with God-talk. Commentator Brevard Childs: "Of course, a tremendous anthropomorphism is involved, but the extreme caution with which it is used is an eloquent testimony to the Hebrew understanding of God."

In the Heidelberg dispute the passage comes to be used metaphorically for the God who remains hidden but is also disclosed in the cross of Jesus Christ. Like Moses, we can only see God from the rear, never directly. In fact, the God one wishes to see face to face keeps receding, as it were. God is revealed in the gurgling and helpless infant of Bethlehem, the crier of dereliction, "My God, my God, why hast Thou forsaken me," in the weakness of one on the cross, in the dying and dead Christ.

Here is where tremendous and crude anthropomorphism gives rise to startling and confusing paradox: the revealed God also remains hidden. God reveals, but only faith sees, so God is concealed at the very time of disclosure. No human contemplation, speculation, reasoning, gazing at the wonders of creation, or moral achievement assures any part of the direct or head-on view of God. An Isaiah text always comes into play: "Truly you are a hidden God" (Is. 45:15). When God reveals, it is through weakness, through suffering and thus veiled except to the eye of faith, a mysterious eye for which I cannot account.

A second last twist in this "God and me" relation is as jarring as are all the others. It would be so easy, so comforting to talk, if one could claim a glimpse of the face of God, some sure and secure experience. Instead, in this tradition, since all depends upon faith, there is no room for "claiming." Whenever I read about people whose experience of God still leaves them with a tinge of doubt, a tad of despair, a smidgeon of uncertainty, something possibly to be overcome, soon to be bypassed, I have to say: all those elements are there from the beginning and remain to the end. They are basic to the structure of the experience of God, not deterrents, hurdles, embarrassments, accidents, or momentary diversions.

Instead, in this grasp of the experience of or language about God, there is an understanding that it is God who attacks the human with doubts, who undercuts human achievements, including those of the spiritual sort. It is not "original sin" or "the devil" or "the structures of evil" that lie at the root, but God who sends *Anfechtungen* (the technical term; now forget it). God does this "killing" in order to give life, destroys this blighted "old creation" in order to bring in the "new creation." So Luther can speak of this experience—get used to paradox—as "delicious despair." That deliciousness is not of the sort designed to appeal to the masochist. It is delicious because of its intention and outcome: the disclosing of God.

Martin E. Marty

Two things that neither this nor any other God-talk has done, is doing, or will do. First, it cannot wheel out on stage, as it were, and subject to empirical analysis some object called "God." Second it cannot provide a philosophically satisfying answer to the problem of evil.

All God-talk occurs between the absence of the first object and the presence of the second problem. In the "hind parts of God" approach, however, evil and suffering are not accidental and meaningless disruptions. They are integral to the experience of God who comes, as God did and does in Jesus Christ, in the midst of suffering and in the presence of the face of evil. The result of the encounter is not to damn but to save, not to blind but to cause seeing, not to keep God distant but to bring God close.

McGrath quotes Luther on this theme in respect to the vocation of the theologican: "living, or rather dying and being damned make a theologian, not understanding, reading or speculating." I am aware of what a slight misreading of one half of all this paradoxical thought can lead to, has often led to. This talk about "killing" or reducing or humbling the aspiring human might indeed appeal to the masochist, the person who lacks and wants to lack self-esteem. Without going into detail, let me only mention that instead, since everything is now thrown upon the revealing power of a loving and saving God in whom one trusts, faith relies on the promise that this God will "make alive." And this reliance leads people in this tradition, including me, to speak in the highest possible terms about the self-esteem of a person who trusts in this suffering, crucified God. Viewed from the angle of the saving God, the same person who is otherwise impotent, evil, "killed," is also powerful, good, alive. This person is to be seen "as" Christ and even as "a" Christ to the neighbor and in the world.

That positive remark represents quite a leap in the plot, so it is necessary to do some retracing now.

Is there nothing one "knows" about the hidden God from the experience of nature, creation, or from human reason? There are some biblical clues to traces written into the heart of conscience. The same Marty who can experience his own raw a-theism in the face of earthquake and holocaust, the vision of hungry bellies and the demonism of the mighty, can also experience wonder, gain insight, and relish imagination in respect to these clues and traces. Like so many other non-scientists, I have a naive sort of "natural theology" that has its own place, but does not overcome the hiddenness of God.

So I like to share something of Pascal's and Kant's sense of infinite spaces, and I make a kind of hobby reading about universes. Let me bore you by enjoying, as I often do, thinking about something gleaned from a chess encyclopedia: that if two players simply set out to make all the moves mathematically possible on a chessboard, it would take them a long time: there are as many possibilities as there are believed to be neutrons in our universe. Infinite, shall we say? If so much contingency comes with one chess board, think what comes with six billion brains, each with trillions of cells. I try to think about what "chance" in the natural evolutionary process it takes to produce the retina in one rat eye. The "Big Bang" notion and what occurs in a millimillisecond is quickening, and inspires God-thought if not God-talk. And yet, and yet: none of that

Martin E. Marty

moves one beyond the hidden God, for which I know no name. Is such a God responsive? Does she have a name? Where do I direct thought and prayer? So, not being chartered to be a cosmologist, I can only say that such reflection helps keep me from rendering God small, or young. Not much more.

The God of the cosmos takes on meaning, in this tradition, from my childhood Catechism days, when first I saw things cut to size. "I believe in God, . . . the maker of heaven and earth" comes to mean chiefly, "I hold and believe that I am a creature of God; . . . that none of us has his life of himself, . . ." The risks of anthropocentrism in human response, to be sure, matches the medium of anthropomorphism in revelation. Those are worthwhile risks to take: the cosmos is big enough to take care of itself and outbalance any egotism that results from one's thinking personally about the meaning of creation.

And what of a God of Order? One who devotes a life, as I am doing, in no small part to reflecting on religion in a pluralist republic—and opposing theocracy or a legally-titled "Christian America," again then poses civil existence between a-theism or secularity, on one hand, and the Lordship of God in matters of public life and the human polis on the other.

There are not, in this understanding, two Gods, one a God of order and the other a saving God. But there are distinct works and ways by which the one God is apprehended. The one "hidden" God is seen to be active as Lord of history, setting up structures of human existence over which we can argue. That same God is active also among those who do not know, recognize, or accept God, and one may often deal more intimately with them than with some fellow-believers in matters civil. And that same God, once more, is the God who in the story and effects of the suffering and dying Jesus Christ, engages in the sovereign saving activity that we call announcing "the Kingdom of God" and effecting "the forgiveness of sins."

Here is a third element: if the "hind parts of God" come to be known in a particular story, that of Israel and of Jesus on the cross, does that story exhaust God-talk and God-experience? Sooner or later one must get serious about the activity of God among people where this story never has been heard or will be heard. One must reckon with those among the God-seekers and knowers who are remote or, for reasons of their own accidents of birth and cultural experience, who stand outside the scope where this disclosing, this revealing of the hidden, concealed God is witnessed to. What about that range of elements that lies in things between "God and me"?

Let me say first off that I have no more respect for the person who claims to have *this* issue solved than I do for those who claim to have worked out themes classically called "predestination" or "foreknowledge" by God. One only says something because the mind must be active, something calls for a responsible address. It may be that anything said is like St. Augustine said talk about the Trinity had to be: slightly better than mere silence. As one sets out here, mere silence sometimes seems preferable to words. Yet, one sets out. How would I begin to? The step is as hazardous as those that have gone before.

Martin E. Marty

Above I mentioned a "second last twist" in what this concept of the hidden God entailed. Now for a last one in the overall scheme which will still demand elaboration. McGrath, better than most, has shown how the "hidden God" notion means two things. First, *Deus absconditus* is the God who is hidden *in* God's revelation. This God is identical with the *Deus revelatus*, the God revealed in suffering, weakness, and folly. One looks at the same events and sees both aspects of God. In the cross one sees a wrathful and at the same time merciful God; faith grasps the merciful God. So far, so good.

In this reading, however, *Deus absconditus*, the hidden God, is hidden not only *in* but also *behind* God's revelation. What does this mean? Once more we visit a moment in intellectual history, in its own way as perplexing as the Heidelberg Disputation. This time it finds Luther hassling with Erasmus over "the bound" or "the free" will. The argument contends that along with the revealed God, there are dimensions of God's activity which are and always will remain hidden from us.

In this context Martin Luther did the scariest thing he ever did, intellectually, but once the thought reaches a Christian, it seems to me that no one can take serious any God-talk that does not at least passingly let this motif threaten. McGrath puts in succinctly, so let us keep depending on him for guidance through the Erasmus debate. Now the *Deus absconditus*, the hidden God, the one known only through the view of the "back side," is also understood as the God who must in some dimensions remain forever unknown to us (in history, I would say). God in this prospect is possibly a "mysterious and sinister being whose intentions remain concealed from us."

One must concede the possibility of a concealed *(occulta)* will of God. There is more to God than we can know from God's self-revelation. All this is more likely a problem of our perception than a statement of how things are, but the possibility has to be reckoned with that "behind the merciful God who is revealed in the cross of Christ there may well be a hidden God whose intentions are diametrically opposite."

Existentially, this is what keeps little Lutheran kids awake. Hence, Nietzsche?

Again existentially, this might be what a Lutheran grown up might get lost in in Henri Nouwen's prescribed contemplative retreat. Hence, Marty's chill at dinner?

Theologically, this notion is what threatens, as McGrath puts it, to make "theology an irrelevancy, if any statements which can be made on the basis of divine revelation may be refuted by appealing to a hidden and inscrutable God, whose will probably contradicts that of the revealed God." Let it be said that Luther got himself into this perplexing position in the course of a tortuous argument over free will that he wanted to win against Erasmus; that he lost his moorings from his own notion that the cross alone was his theology; that it was a rare and minor and passing theme; that he more steadily took the advice of his Augustinian confessor, Johannes von Staupitz, in such matters: on subjects of this sort, do not try to proceed from the unknown to the known, but from the known to the unknown. Not: did God predestine the abandonment of any creature,

Martin E. Marty

including, notably, "me"? Not: might the inscrutable, nonrevealing God have designs that conflict with the loving revelation? But instead: look at what is known, at the wounds of Christ, the cross as a mark of suffering love, the reality of the new creation as seal of God's triumph in our lives.

Even as one turns from the edge of that abyss, however, it has always seemed worthwhile to me to compensate by turning it around, as well. Does it make me an indomitable "positive thinker" to say that just as the *Deus absconditus*, the hidden God, can be understood as unknown, mysterious, and sinister, can this same God not also be understood as not-yet-known, potentially revealing, benign in extending encompassing love beyond "the story" of Exodus or the Gospels? Critics would call the notion implied by this question a soft "universalism."

Another way to put that: if the first word in theology is universalism, that we are all in different boats heading for the same shore, that it does not make any difference what one believes so long as one believes, or whether one believes or not, then there can be no moral or spiritual or theological rigor to the search. Witnessing to the encompassing "universal" love of God comes in as a last word, among people who have taken the story of *Deus revelatus*, the God revealed in Israel and Jesus, in Bible and Church, with utter seriousness. Then one commends the Hindu with her stories, the Buddhist with his "Holy Emptiness" where "God" would be, the agnostic who has not yet found the signals of God compelling, to the tender mercies of the God whose "hind parts" we know in the glimpses in stories of

111

Sinai, Calvary, and other mountains and the people on them.

Those brink-throughts, abyss-experiences, highrisk-expressions are backgrounds, however, to the more ordinary experience of and witness to God hidden, God revealed. Just as Alice in Wonderland could believe six impossible things before breakfast, I can go through six breakfasts without having to dwell on such impossible things. Most of the time relations between "God and me" are executed not on the highwires of reflection but on the plain ground of dailiness.

No doubt all who respond to the editor of this book are expected to say something about the living out of the experience, the working out of "the story." One does this not in the spirit of "let me tell you about my operation" or "my foreign trip," or "here is how you should do it." More likely—at least I find it so when I do my spiritual "hitchhiking"—we listen to each other, compare notes, and ask what it means to be related to God now, not in the time of Moses or Jesus or Erasmus.

First, the experience of God occurs more in community than in solitariness. Of course, I believe in the value of solitude along with its inevitability. One dies "by one's self" and believes "for one's self." Each of us has a world, is a world, and has irreplaceable personal needs, blights, delights. To believe otherwise would be to shirk responsibility, to miss the intrinsic value of experiences, to deny the integrity of biblical witness to the value of each person of the covenant—in Christian terms, each named baptized one. We are taught, and I relish the thought of it still, that in the Eucharist, the most important words are "given and shed *for you.*" It is not egotistic thus to think, but a failure to grasp what seriousness and grace are all about if one does not.

Having said that, however, one returns quickly to the notion of community. The spiritual biographies of Moses, the disciples of Jesus, Augustine or Staupitz, Luther or Erasmus, are compelling but not determining. They are important as part of the *Qehal Yahweh,* the congregation of Yahweh; of the church as the Body of Christ. In the Hebrew Scriptures not to be "of the people" was damnation, and to be "of the people" or "a people" was a making whole.

Here again, the primal experience of this person who never outgrew his Catechism and does not try to outgrow it reflects thus on more of the Creed. "I believe in the Holy Spirit, the holy Catholic church..." means: the Holy Spirit "first leads us into his holy community, placing us upon the bosom of the church, where he preaches to us and brings us to Christ." No word there about the Protestant "right of private judgment" being first. The Holy Spirit "has a unique community in the world. It is the mother that begets and bears every Christian through the Word of God." More: "I believe that there is on earth a little holy flock or community of pure saints under one head, Christ....Of this community I also am a part and member, a participant and co-partner in all the blessings it possesses."

For me this means that the Eucharist and daily recall of Baptism (which "incorporates" one into Christ and thus into life with God) are more immediate, nurturing, and empowering than contemplation, meditation, or private prayer. To whisper a prayer in the company of others in East Germany, to have the sacrament with an ecumenical group on a slope toward Jerusalem and "the upper room," to plead with God for justice in a congregation of blacks in South Africa, to huddle against the oblivious environment in a little church in Japan and, week after week, to participate in "intercessions" for the ill, the tempted, the triumphant in our home parish—all these suit me more than private prayer.

Lifelong, I have read the injunctions to rise to prayer for an hour or two in the morning. At fifty New Years and a thousand new days I have made resolutions to follow the discipline, only soon to fail. When I hear the thunk-thunk of two newspapers hitting the front porch at 5:40 a.m., I make the sign of the cross to token baptism, new life, resurrection, may read a page of Moravian daily devotions, and am then roused to an hour of reading in the newspapers about the world in which God is hidden and revealed.

King James Version psalms serve as table graces because through them one experiences ancient language of prayer, voiced world-wide, though I welcome impromptu prayers by those gifted to say them. And, yes, later in the day prayer is usually of the "hitch-hiking" sort. It helps my dull kind to tag along with the language of Dorothy Day or Mother Teresa, Meister Eckardt or Dom Helder Camara, Dag Hammarskjold or Charles Peguy.

Of course, there are arrow prayers, stabs at the heart of God hidden and revealed. These can be petitions, ask-

Martin E. Marty

ings-for, or thanks for graces received. I'd like to think of
myself as quite conventional in these respects. There have
been seasons of intense suffering in the family circle,
moments of sheer terror as I imagine myself in the cancer
ward, eucharistic bedazzlements as when a child was born,
esthetic eruptions while singing Bach, and each of these
occasions something-like-prayer.

What does one expect in each? How does one think of
answers? From childhood on, and perhaps more every
year, I am puzzled or put off by people who know exactly
what the hidden God is doing for them. When four marines
survive an attack that kills hundreds and one hears them
and their families talking about God's choice of them, a
special providence, I only feel for and think with the
parents who become ragers against God who must, in that
case, have been left out. When I hear someone say that
God took special loving care to spare her because a traffic
jam kept her from reaching a fatal air flight, this only
makes the problem of theodicy worse for the survivors of
those who went down with the plane when it crashed or
with me standing by and looking on.

Somewhere I once read of a different notion of prayer.
The model was not one of petition that would be satisfied
only if one "got what she wanted" or that was resigned
to "thy will be done." Instead, one overheard Jesus in the
Garden of Gethsemane—see how far the hiddenness of God
goes in the act of revelation?—praying that the cup of suffering be removed. He would pray, repeatedly, "not my
will, but thine, be done." In one of the accounts we read,
"And there appeared to him an angel from heaven,

115

strengthening him." Then? "And being in an agony he prayed more earnestly; . . ." And then? "And when he rose from prayer" he chided disciples into activity and went out to meet the task before him.

The scholar who alerted me to this spoke of a kind of "concurrent communication" that one has with God, as between parent and child, wife and husband. You are in a constant if often quiet conversation, and know roughly what the other is to say or do. The eight-year-old might ask for a Jaguar or the Taj Mahal for Christmas, but at age eight she should have some sense of scope about the parental response. The same child might ask for roller skates and have a little more sense of communication, concerning the range of prospects, limits, bargaining, and the like.

When the body is wracked with cancer cells and most vital organs are gone, one prays not for a miracle that would reverse the deterioration—oh, I know, some do—but instead that "nothing shall separate us from the love of God in Christ Jesus." Nothing does. Love is stronger than death; that is the witness of many who have trusted in the hidden, also revealed, God who appears in the midst of suffering.

After prayer, I will mention preaching, verbal communication, Christian conversation. I am often drawn close to God when things go right as a homilist exegetes a biblical text and applies it to our times. "Faith comes by hearing" is a Pauline notion engraved in the traditions of our expectations. "In the beginning was the Word." Mine is a Word-centered (God-speak, Christ as Logos, Scripture as witness, and then "preached") faith. If I knew more about the mystery of faith and why preaching quickens it in some and dulls it in others (or why some preachers can help kill it off or make it live), I would say more. For now, I listen.

Similarly, I am what E. L. Mascall called a "eucharistic type" person. In the midst of a world of agony, there are signs of a Presence, seen in the gathered congregation receiving the bread and the cup. On a day when the homily fails, the meal often brings this vivid sense of connection. I have never had a mystical experience and do not seek it. That ought to be clear from what went before. But I have a baptismal and eucharistic piety which brings its own sense of the Presence, of God still hidden when revealed in the sacramental acts. But present.

Along with the concept of "God and me" in community and in prayer, in preaching and sacraments, there is—at least for this pragmatic, action-theory-oriented (a little jargon, please!) American, also a sense of the presence of God in the sphere of human action. The hidden God is revealed in the face of the person in need, in the struggles of the oppressed, in the endeavors of, yes, the middle class who might also be stirred by the God who reveals. I mentioned Charles Peguy before. Recall his "Everything begins in mysticism and ends in politics." For Moses this meant first the Sinaitic vision of the "hind parts" of God and then, down the mountain, leadership in the politics of Israel.

The notion of a God who reveals not a splendid face but only the hind parts equips one to sense the presence in a spouse who spends years suffering with, defying, and outlasting the alcoholism. Here, as always, there is not a clarified, unambiguous face. The structures of evil pervade existence, and will continue to, no matter what our stories or prayers, until the end of history. Yet one sees signs of the Gracious Other in the acts of the Gracious Brother and Sister. The crucified God suffers in the midst of the world, and the believing community witnesses to this presence by responsive activity.

As in the case of individual suffering and being spared, I am reluctant to be too specific again about the "here" and "there" of that which signals God's activity. Both sides in wars and in politics are ready to overclaim God on their side. Must one be sure that his side is in absolute congruence with God's will? One has to act on the basis of what can be known, can be calculated. Still, in the sphere of activity one finds the path of holiness and the means of serving the Holy One.

God and me: what does one do about the relation? In Israel and in Christendom the witness to this hidden God/revealed God once seemed to be transferred with the genes and the territory, as it were. One acquired faith from the tradition of elders and passed it on without reflecting on the only choice in town. Modernity has undercut tradition and community, and there is very little genetic or territorial transfer of faith. The evangelistic Protestant communities are the true moderns, for they have caught on to that, while Catholic Christianity languishes relatively in cultures like those in Western Europe and North America.

I believe that we are all accidentally and casually "evangelists," whether for Mercedes-Benz or Blue Moun-

Martin E. Marty

tain Coffee, for the best-sellers of our choice or habits and preferences in life. So, in a way, our understandings of God get emitted by the choices we make and the things we say about them. It seems that one can both respect what the hidden God may have in store for people who are very different, engaging in dialogue with them for the sake of a common humanity *and*, in certain circumstances, in turn be explicit about "the story" of God's way in Christ, or in explaining actions that issue from it. In other words, we are, most of us, writing "God and me" plots much of the time.

I do not think this means that one must convert all circumstances into compulsive constellations for witness. Gabriel Marcel speaks of a reprehensible image of God as a God of "prey and pounce," as it were. This image of God appears if we all wait for the moment of someone else's weakness and try to replace all that they are and have with a packaged version of our story. One is not merely passive in dealing with the Presence, but one need not be imperial or triumphalist, either.

When a person experiences something of grace in the midst of the puzzles and suffering, when one comes to have some sort of trust in a God who reveals a specific character, he or she develops a quiet confidence. This means, for me in the context of God and me, a contentment with what gets one through the day and what gets one through the life. A word about each is in order.

Getting through the day: the relations between God and me, weak at times and expressive at others, seem to run only strong enough to last through the present day. As for

119

the present day, my understanding of "God and me" accents the concept of vocation, with a strong interest in dailiness. This sense means that what I am called to today has my name on it, expects my distinctive stamp, is a way of serving out the purposes of God. To be free for it, the key element is that I carry no burden from the past or for the future. Of course, psychologically, one inevitably does. Yet there is in this theology much impetus and some equipment for clearing the agenda.

If my trust in what is revealed of the hidden God is sure, I have no reason for guilt about yesterday, or worry about tomorrow. Even to be aware of the "no reason for" is a step toward therapeutic expressions of it. By personality type or theological affirmation or disciplined grasp, I have tried to refuse to be or feel guilty. The morningly sign of the cross and the recall of baptism, the repentance for the old and the resurrection of the New Being "today"—all this means that in this story that "mysterious and sinister" remote God whose face I cannot see has moved now not only with a protective hand over the cleft in the rock where I hide, but also an erasing one. This act of god, which we call "forgiveness" or the disclosure of New Being invites me to entertain a mode of acting and thinking that frees me for what the day can bring.

As for tomorrow—and here my address is less complete—I am not to worry, but to repose confidence in the trustworthiness of God, who calls from tomorrow, from the future. A quick personal accounting: several years ago, during the deepest spiritual and emotional agonies of my life. I would swing onto the expressway in the darkness before dawn to take up the day's task. At that time, it included hours spent in a hospital visit. The word "terminal" had been pronounced over an illness. And I would each morning in that earliest hour think darker thoughts that foresaw, that day, no dawn that was coming.

In the midst of them I undertook disciplines. Did these dark thoughts have to do with *this* day? Some of them, part of each of them, may have. But most of them tried to focus on mysterious, sinister events and forces that belonged to nameless, undefined future days. About them I could do nothing. And, what was more: we had not so clearly been promised strength to face occurrences in such futures. We pray for our "daily" bread. We are to take no thought for the morrow. This is not a story about happy endings, but about strength for the day. I keep trying to learn with the heart what the head knows: that I can do little about finitude, contingency, and transcience, as these respect tomorrows. At best, I can address today, and that is enough.

And, getting through life. It unsettles me a bit that I cannot tantalize the reader with stories of great breaches, astounding discoveries, born again delights, total enlightenments. In our epoch these are often advertised as entitlements for Everyperson. Is it not a sign of stubborn, static existence in one who, as I do, keeps resorting to a matrix formed in childhood, a template cut out of Catechism, an at-homeness within the tradition in which one was born?

The historian in me relishes both continuity, of which there has been some, and disruption or change, of which there has been more than this account might suggest. Yet I prefer metaphors of growth-in-context to those that hint that one can jump out of one's skin, be "into" this year and that year and still have a core or center to personal and social existence.

This commitment results from the sense I draw from the chessboard and its infinite numbers of games, from all the potentials for interactions and the possibilities of new ideas growing out of what was handed down: tradition. While nurtured within a context of continuity, there has been very little shelter in my chosen (= vocation) academic, intellectual, political, editorial, and spiritual life. That calling takes me, yes, also by choice, to the junctures where the religious meets the secular in pluralistic conjunctions. No shelter there. But I have found precisely at such junctures that the people who endure best are those who are deeply rooted. Gandhi. King. Buber. Merton. Bonhoeffer. Day. Naude. John XXIII. We picture them drawing constant sustenance from a particular community and vision of reality—and then being free to respond to others' ways, to be empathic about people for whom "God and me" would sound like a very different story than does their own.

We are pilgrims together, in the end—are we not?— necessarily content, in this life and these years—with the "hind parts" or "back side" of a God revealed. This God, unless we would put limits on what God means and thus on God, is ahead of us, beckoning from the future, ready to reveal more in the midst of "finitude, contingency, and transcience."

MY LAST CONFESSION

John Deedy

LOOKING back, my faith—we're being confessional here, right?—has evolved dramatically from that which was passed on to me by my parents, born Catholics both of them, then fostered by Sisters of Notre Dame de Namur through the eight formative grade-school years; it has evolved from the faith that was furthered by the Xaverian Brothers through four years of high school, then honed by the Jesuits at Holy Cross College; it has evolved from the faith that was mine when I entered religious journalism back in 1951. That's almost four decades of evolution.

The bottom line is not that I believe more, or even that I believe less, but rather that I believe differently. *I've evolved.* The "God-and-me" relationship of my sixty-fourth year is different from the "God-and-me" relationship of the person who marched in parish May processions; who served Mass dutifully for years; who went through college initialing the top of blue-book tests "A.M.D.G."—initials of the Jesuit motto, *Ad Majorem Dei Gloriam,* "To the Greater Glory of God." My faith is different from that of the John Deedy, the diocesan editor who covered a Vatican Council twenty years ago; the John Deedy, who was managing editor at *Commonweal* going on a dozen years; the John Deedy, who in the course of four decades has written for scores of Catholic publications, and originated or contributed to several books of explicit Catholic definition. I've evolved. My faith has evolved. And so has that of my Catholic co-religionists—for some, again, in ways they may not even realize.

In recent years I've asked Catholic friends in various contexts what they perceive as different about their faith today—how it has evolved from the faith of their youth. Mostly I've heard answers dwelling on the vernacular, the "new" Mass, the displacement of private devotions, the emphases on hymn singing, and the like. But when you come right down to it, responses of this sort are mostly superficial, involving faith and religious practice at the surface level. Substantively, the answers do not signal a whole lot. Neither do certain other changed aspects of the faith as lived and encountered nowadays, like the fewer number of people in the pews, or fewer religious vocations, or most any other changed existential Catholic situation that springs to mind.

What clues me that faith and one's duties as a Catholic, thus one's God and me relationship, are perceived differently these days—mine as much as the next person's—is the decline of the sacrament that we grew up knowing as confession or penance, and now call the sacrament of reconciliation. This sacrament is in a state of near extinction—not just because fewer Catholics are the zealous, conscientious practitioners of the faith that they once were, but rather because many Catholics, the most conscientious included, have obviously assimilated into their spiritual lives a different notion about what constitutes sin and what

John Deedy

one should do to obtain forgiveness. This is a radical development in the Catholic church. Certainly it is in my life as a Catholic.

In the halcyon days of flourishing vocations, contented religious, thriving parochial schools and crowded church parking lots on Sunday mornings, confession ranked as a kind of fifth mark of American Catholicism for most Catholics. Weekly, bi-weekly and seldom less frequently than once a month, we queued up Saturdays in confessional lines between the hours of four-to-six and seven-to-nine p.m., and examined conscience as we patiently awaited our turn to enter that darkened confessional box where a priest listened to sins and absolved us of guilt before God. For the average Catholic, myself included, the Saturday confession was almost as much ritual as the Sunday communion—until some time in the late 1960s. Then, the winds that blew away vocations, unsettled many religious, shook the schools and opened up spaces in church parking lots suddenly wiped out confessional lines. It was as if a tornado had struck. Overnight, the hallowed practice of confessing one's sins before a priest became a thing of the past for most American Catholics—certainly a huge percentage at least. Saturday's confessional period was telescoped in most places to a half hour or less, and the hours once set aside for this sacrament were replaced by Saturday's Masses of anticipation—late afternoon and early evening liturgies which extend the time frame for fulfillment of the Sunday obligation.

Saturday's Masses of anticipation are a welcome, blessed innovation. But the eclipse of confession as a popular sacramental staple of Catholic spirituality remains a startling circumstance. From time immemorial the church had fostered confession, doing so in what it regarded as a keeping of the prescription of Matthew 16:19 (". . . whatsoever you loose on earth shall be loosed in heaven"), and means of restoring to individual lives the grace and holiness forfeited by grievous sins. But suddenly Catholics by the tens of thousands were deciding for themselves that they did not need to utilize this process in their religious lives. Nor did this seem some uniquely American phenomenon. In country after country across Christendom Catholics were quitting the practice of confessing regularly. What had happened?

The New York Times noted the phenomenon, and fifteen or so years ago asked me to do a piece on the subject. In due course the piece examining the waning popularity among Catholics of confessing to a priest in the confessional appeared in the *Times'* Week-in-Review Section. I dug out my file clipping recently, and the one-dimensionality of my analysis embarrassed me mightily. Essentially, I saw Catholics embracing the Protestant practice of confessing sins directly to God, and quoted a priest to the effect that there was probably an inevitability about this. "The individual is still his own best mediator before God," I quoted the priest as saying. "He doesn't need my ear."

"Mediator" appeared as "editor," because of a *Times* typographical error, but that is today the smallest part of my embarrassment. I feel embarrassment because so much more was involved in the issue, so much more was taking place in the lives of Catholics than what I indicated. Since

John Deedy

most interpretative writing and analysis tends to be highly subjective, my *Times* clipping tells me that I was unaware even of what was taking place in my own life as Catholic and believer. Not that I was being dishonest or personally uncommunicative. I was just—well, kind of blind to things.

I overlooked completely, for instance, the possibility that Catholics—again, myself included—might be adopting an entirely new perspective not only about sin, but about the God who sits in the heavens, and that this new perspective radically affected, if not the quality of one's faith, then most certainly the manner in which this faith was being lived out in the modern Catholic situation. Specifically, the God of Judgment, the all-seeing, all-knowing God who would one day demand an account of the individual's whole life, every thought, word, act of commission and deed of omission—that God was dead, a caricature, an artifact from one's religious childhood. That God of judgment had been replaced by a God of love and forgiveness, a God of mercy, a God who, in a word, was generous and open-armed rather than strictly retributive according to a detailed code constructed over centuries by those who acted as this God's representatives on earth. When the old God went out, out went many of the old concepts of sin, beginning with "sins" of the type invented just so we'd have something to fill the silence of the confessional. In time, out went confession itself, and a new personalist tradition took root in the Catholic Church, one that stressed the very element which is the title of this book, "God and Me."

My conviction that the "God and me" personalist approach constituted the new, broad reality among Catholics was strengthened recently when I interviewed a score or more Catholics on their conceptions of the last judgment. The interviewing was done for an article for *U.S. Catholic*, and before starting the interviewing I allowed myself a presumption or two. The principal one was that my subjects would hold the idea of a last judgment in awe and look ahead to the experience with a certain trepidation about what the event held in store for them. I couldn't have been more mistaken. Only two, a husband and wife, among the twenty-five or thirty interviewed believed they would come before God for a strict accounting. Most expressed a degree of skepticism that there actually would be a last judgment, while the doubtful harbored the opinion that such judging as did occur was not particularly to be feared, as it was not likely to result in one's being punished since God was too good and forgiving to be dispatching people willy-nilly to eternal damnation.

These were all life-long, practicing Catholics, yet except for two of them, the old juridical concept of a God rewarding and punishing according to some detailed balance sheet was more quaint than probable. Nearly all felt that personal failings really meant little except in some context of the larger society, to which all felt strong responsibilities. No one, for instance, literally believed that reward or punishment awaited because the letter of the church's moral code had been observed or not. They did not feel, in sum, that human decree was going to bind in the hereafter.

Now admittedly I talked to a relatively small sampling

of people, only a few of whom had theological credentials of a professional kind. Their views could all be as wrong-headed as a malfunctioning traffic light. Nonetheless, they were a representative cross section of the people in the pews in my part of the world, and however exotic some of their theories, somehow in their composite selves I saw myself. Thus it was that that *U.S. Catholic* writing assignment became for me something of an exercise in religious and spiritual self-discovery. If nothing more, through those persons I came to understand better my own attitude toward confession, among other things, and with this came a concomitant understanding of my current relationship to God.

In other words, in the religious and spiritual sphere I had gone through a series of changes. Take confession: I had evolved from a Catholic who had "hit the box" weekly, often with a silly litany of supposed sins ("Father, I missed my night prayers three times; I swore ten times ...etc."), to a Catholic who confesed maybe once or twice a year, to a Catholic who quit the confessional entirely, yet who does not feel any more removed from God for having done so.

The last time I went to confession was, I think, back around 1970; I'd have to check an old passport for the exact year. I was going to Moscow, and airplanes being airplanes, Moscow being Moscow and all, and a long way off to boot, I thought it advisable to review affairs of conscience and get some things in order before leaving. I took myself to confession at a church on Park Avenue in Manhattan. It had been almost two years since my last confession, and around 1970 that was still a long time between appearances in the confessional. The priest immediately seized on the time gap, and asked why it had been so long since my last confession. In awkward and, I recall, painful truthfulness I explained that one reason was because the priest who had been my regular confessor, a close personal friend, had left the active ministry, and I hadn't replaced him as confessor with anyone else. I wasn't quite prepared for the response. The priest hearing my confession suddenly began to pour out a confession to me. He concluded that I was demoralized, and I concluded in return that whether I was demoralized or not he definitely was. He began to anguish with me, and before I knew it I was hearing, if not exactly his confession, then his baring of heart and soul. It was an unnerving experience— role reversal at the most intimate and surprising of levels. It was the last thing in the world I was prepared for, and frankly it helped establish another time gap in my appearance in a confessional box.

In fact, as I mentioned a few paragraphs back, I haven't been back to a confessional box since. The reason why has nothing to do over the long run with the experience on Park Avenue. That affected me profoundly, but not forever after. Certainly it does not begin to account for a distancing effect of seventeen or eighteen years.

I haven't been back to confession, because like so many of those Catholics, of my *U.S. Catholic* article, I have personalized my relationship with God, or at least have de-institutionalized it to considerable degree. I really don't think I believe much differently from before, and, confession apart, I practice my religion pretty much now as

John Deedy

in the past. I observe the Sunday obligation rigorously, for instance. I make it to Mass on the holy days, and I contribute to the support of my pastor. So it isn't that I've decided to walk alone or that I've totally internalized belief. I belong to the Catholic community and my relationship with God still has a strong community element about it. That suits me fine.

To the extent, however, that confession is important in the Catholic scheme of things, I suppose I'm a different Catholic. But a point to be emphasized: My abandonment—or, more accurately, my neglect of formal sacramental confession—is not to be understood as some rebellious acting out or reactionary expression of behavioral independence from ritual or from the church's prescribed code of religious practice. It isn't for me, nor do I think it is for many others like me. For most Catholics *real* sin is still sin. What's different is that I, as no doubt many other Catholics, have different thoughts, thoughts of our own, about where sins or transgressions of a problem kind have to be taken.

Here, I think, the revised liturgy of the Mass has itself become a factor in my religious evolution, at least so far as confession is concerned—though likely affected in due course is my entire relationship with God. The new Mass becomes involved specifically through the penitential rite which follows immediately after the entrance antiphon and greeting at all Masses celebrated according to the revised ritual. Several forms of penitential rite may be used, of course, but whichever one the celebrant chooses, expressly and implicitly involved for me are the elements of sacramental confession itself: confession of sin, expression of regret, and forgiveness from God.

Admittedly, though not pointedly designated as such, a penitential rite was part of the old Mass in the prayers at the foot of the altar—the priest-celebrant reciting the Confiteor and the acolyte, representative of the congregation, responding with a Confiteor of his own (no female acolytes then), word for word the same as the priest's. But this was all in Latin, and the actuality of a penitential rite, its meaning and implication, were largely lost in the mumble and garble of hurried execution in a language no one understood, except maybe the priest.

Today the Mass, including the penitential rite, takes place in a language that we all understand. As for the penitential rite, it is often preceded by an explanation of purpose by the priest, followed by a few moments of silence so that individuals may review and resolve to amend the sinful sides of their selves. It is understood, of course, that this rite is not general absolution (although some priests apparently have used the ritual on occasion as such). Nonetheless, the effect of the rite is to satisfy me and seemingly a number of other Catholics that under ordinary circumstances it is such confession of sins as is necessary, and they accept the priest's concluding response ("May almighty God have mercy on us, forgive us our sins, and bring us to life everlasting") as the intoning of a type of absolution.

Saturday confession may, in effect, have gone the way of Friday abstinence, but its place has been taken by a penitential rite within the sacrament of the Mass, and this rite within a liturgy seems to satisfy the spiritual need very

many Catholics feel for forgiveness from sin. I know it does
me.

It is not that I have become, to return to the garbled
word of my *Times* piece, my own mediator before God,
Protestant fashion. The penitential rite of the Mass has that
necessary element which in my view continues to set me
as Catholic off from other Christians so far as sin and divine
forgiveness are linked in necessary sequential connection.
For the penitential rite of the new liturgy of the Mass involves the presence and the participation of the priest. The
common Protestant penitential tradition, in my understanding, is to confess one's sins directly to God and to
realize forgiveness in one's own conscience. That, I hasten
to say, is not what I have evolved to, for so far as I am
concerned it is not what the penitential rite of the Mass
is all about. The penitential rite of the new Mass involves
the priest, though admittedly the rite may sometimes be
led by a deacon. But deacon or priest, there is a clerical
presence and for me this is of crucial importance. The priest
(citing him, since he's generally the one involved) intro-
duces the rite; and it is the priest who intones the plea for
forgiveness and the related hope that those who are a part
of the liturgy will be brought to eternal life.

What I'm saying, for whatever difference it makes, is
that, though I have bypassed formal sacramental confession, I have not bypassed the priest and the confession
which the priest makes possible within the celebration of
the liturgy. That may sound convoluted, but it satisfies me
spiritually and intellectually. The realization of personal
sin and the necessity to seek its forgiveness are now as ever

in the past very much a part of my "God-and-me" relationship. The fact that I haven't put in an appearance in the confessional box going on twenty years really does not translate to basic change in me as Catholic believer—or as one who feels a spiritual need to confess, for that matter.

I may as well "confess" at this point that, as I don't confess my sins in the same way as in the past, neither do I pray the same way either. There's a small digression I might make in explaining this development in my life. When *The Catholic Fact Book,* a book of mine, appeared in 1986 it was speared by a priest-editor in California for alleged unawareness of contemporary spirituality—a shortcoming betrayed, the critic contended, by the book's reproducing certain traditional prayers, prayers which, in the critic's view, qualified as "museum pieces." The priest-editor did not specifically state which prayers were "museum-pieces," but I suppose they were prayers like the Memorare or the Acts of Faith, Hope and Love. Well, maybe some of the prayers were "museum pieces," but maybe that's only because they're not on that particular priest's agenda of prayers. The truth is that several of the book's prayers are not on mine either. But they do belong to the prayer life of some Catholics. I say that because most of the prayers appearing in the book were included at the suggestion of Catholics consulted in the course of the book's preparation. Also, virtually every one of the prayers included in the book can be found in the back pages of the disposable seasonal missalettes placed in the pews of American Catholic churches. That's where I culled many of them from, as a matter of fact. If *The Catholic Fact Book* included "museum-piece" prayers, then obviously so do some if not all of the officially-approved booklets currently being made available these days to Catholics.

It is not my intention to turn this essay into a debate with a captious priest-editor. The priest-editor seems to prefer spontaneous prayer, and, though my obstinate side is reluctant to concede him anything, I must admit so do I. In fact, apart from the parish liturgy, spontaneous prayer is the basis of my prayer life. Most of the time I *talk* with God rather than recite formal prayers to him—or is God a she? Whatever, if God's up there, seeing all and hearing all, he or she must welcome, occasionally at least, informal, conversational prayer as a change from prayers machine-gunned on high, as it were, by rote. The divine side of God must by now be so weary of "Our Fathers" and "Hail Marys" that even the poorest of human, conversational prayer must be virtually guaranteed a hearing. Or so it seems to me.

In any instance, from me God receives a lot of conversational and informal prayer these days and, by a tactic of mine, prayer that I hope is open-ended. In the old days, many Catholics made the day open-ended in a prayerful way by beginning it with recitation of the "Morning Offering," one of those prayers included in *The Catholic Fact Book* that I suppose the California priest-editor would label a "museum-piece." The "Morning Offering," most Catholics of a certain age will recall, was the prayer through which all "prayers, works, and sufferings" of the day were offered on rising, and thus in advance, to God in thanksgiving for favors, reparation for sins, and a series of other intentions. I used to say the "Morning Offering" religiously—excuse the pun. I haven't said it now for years. My substitution is this: when I pray, formally or otherwise, I use the sign of the cross just once—at the start of my praying and not at the end. This is my replacement method for open-endedness, for being unconsciously in communication with God, for extending the prayerful mode or one's life of prayer beyond the prayer itself.

I don't know where the idea for this system of mine originated. If the idea is owed to any one person specifically, then maybe it is to the late Father H. A. Reinhold, friend and old-church liturgist, whose concepts anticipated so much of the reform of Vatican II. Among other things, Father Reinhold used to advise that people going to Mass bless themselves with holy water on entering church, *but not upon leaving it.* The logic was that the signing of one's self with holy water was the symbolic renewal of the baptismal spirit, and as such had meaning on entering church, which meaning was lost if repeated after Mass and Communion, when the soul was purified by a sacrament greater than the sacramental.

The circumstances and elements are otherwise, but my logic is much the same in my one-way use of the Sign of the Cross when praying. The Sign of the Cross has special meaning at the opening of prayer, and I am anxious for that meaning to carry further, subconsciously or otherwise, after the prayer itself has been broken off. (At the risk of sounding flip, so far as I'm concerned the only time to use the Sign of the Cross at the end of anything nowadays is at the end of most sermons that one hears at Mass, in thanksgiving that they're over. Most sermons are so bad there's little point in their messages carrying beyond the echo.)

And what do I pray for these days? For myself, I admit, and those dear to me. Michael Novak's comment in *Commonweal* of several years ago notwithstanding, the God of "gimme" isn't dead. I look to God for favors, for answers to petitions of a narrowly selfish kind. That admitted, I should say that I also try to make the church's prayers my own, notably those for world peace, peoples of the Third World, and the welfare of humankind generally.

At the same time, and I mean this most sincerely, I pray for the church, and specifically the church in my country, the American Catholic church, that it will retain the loyalty of its people, particularly its young people. In my parish church we pray regularly that "the young people of St. Joachim's will grow up good Catholic citizens." I bristle at that "good Catholic citizens" phrase. It rings for me of church and state, the old God and country syndrome—forever eternal, it would seem in Roman Catholicism, and forever to be suspicious of. Whatever, when I pray for the church, that's not what I'm praying about; that "good Catholic citizens" prayer just doesn't happen to be mine. I really don't worry about the young people of my parish and their citizenship. Indeed, that's probably the least of worries in the parish of our community. The young people of our town, Catholic and otherwise, are going to grow up responsible citizens. They'll raise families, pay their taxes, and vote regularly. I don't worry about any of that, and I don't pray about it. When the prayer is articulated at Mass, which is often, I do not join in the response.

I pray rather that the new generations of American Catholics—my own children included—will stay close to the church, and that those who have placed distance between themselves and the church will draw back to it. I'm not praying for a return to the Catholic yesterdays. I'm not praying for the triumph of orthodoxy, as defined by the papacy of John Paul II. I'm praying rather that the new generations of Catholics will "hang in" as Catholics, and so far as I can tell that prayer is currently not being answered, the recent rash of up-beat assessments of the faith of young adult Catholics notwithstanding. There are enormous reservoirs of good will and commitment, much of it Catholic by explicit definition, in the new generations, and one sees impressive examples of this goodwill and commitment at work in many ways and many places. On the other hand, there is also a startling degree of religious indifference among members of these generations, certainly to the traditions and practices that were virtually instinctive with their parents and grandparents, and that is a concern of mine. I pray for things to change.

Am I unduly alarmist or pessimistic about the new generations of Catholics? I look around me, and wonder.

My wife and I, and those we chum with, are now in the grandparent category. Excusing the truism, the world —more specifically, the church, since that's what we're talking about—belongs increasingly to our children. The so-called baby-boomers are fully launched as the middle generation of adults, many of them with growing families of their own, albeit much smaller families. All of them are fully in charge of decisions and responsibilities into which our generation once had a measure of parental input, but don't now. How are those of them who are Catholic fitting in as Catholics?

Maybe our situation is unusual, but I can think of no family in the circle of friends my wife and I move in where the adult children of the family are all "regularized" in terms of Catholicism and working at it in a systematic way. One or two individuals in a few of the families might be active in what might be called a near-traditional sense, but they constitute the exception. Between second marriages and second thoughts, most of these products of quite orthodox religious upbringing have moved to the fringes of faith or peeled away. They aren't hostile. Most haven't apostatized in the formal sense of having gone and joined some other religion. By and large most still believe, but usually, it seems in some vague sort of way, one that requires neither practice within the institution, nor respect for institutional ways and formulas, nor the institution itself. The requirements of faith have become for them options to be accepted or not, and most of them are rejected, as is the institution.

Recently, for instance, two Catholic friends reported with a mixture of hilarity and matter-of-factness the adventure surrounding the marriage of their daughter. The groom was a young man whom the couple unqualifiedly admire, and they couldn't have been more pleased with the marriage. But, they reported, the marriage ceremony was marked by great complications—and this was the source of the retrospective glee. The ceremony took place on Martha's Vineyard, as planned, but before a justice of the peace, as not planned. No, the priest did not turn up sick and there was no other to be found on the island with proper clerical faculties to marry. A priest was never asked. The justice of the peace presided as one rounded up at the last minute to substitute for a judge, who mysteriously did not show. The story was full of belly laughs. At the end of the story, and almost by way of footnote, the mother of the bride explained that both her daughter and son-in-law were "fallen away." The religious detail was passed on off-handedly, as if their situation was commonplace, no different from that of other Catholic families nowadays. And of course it wasn't. It was only the attending circumstances that varied.

Case histories go on and on.

In a few weeks my wife and I will attend the wedding of the daughter of another set of Catholic friends. Both bride and groom were baptized as Catholics, but the marriage of the two will take place in a rented hall before a civil official. The civil official—the official witness with authority to marry—will be a Catholic. That happens to be the marrying couple's compromise with the Catholic sensitivities of the parents and relatives on both sides of the family.

In similar context, a few weeks ago I had a luncheon reunion with a colleague from days of yore. All four of his children, he volunteered in the course of our mutual up-

John Deedy

dating, are nonpracticing, have drifted into twilight zones of belief.

Catholic magazines occasionally run articles celebrating young people and their commitment to the faith, and my fervent hope is that the articles accurately reflect the church's current situation. But it is not what I am encountering. Those stories of drift and lack of interest repeat themselves almost everywhere my wife and I turn. Sit down with Catholic friends and begin to talk about family—who's married, who isn't; what this child is doing, what's the other doing; who's produced grandchildren and how many of them are there—and conversation eventually swings to the subject of religion. Once upon a time, the subject of the religious state of one's children was never brought up. Their religion was a given, and generally could be a presumed. No longer. Everyone now seems to be telling a tale of self and family, "confessing" as it were to their situation as if in hope of eliciting yours and maybe gaining in the process some oblique consolation that their lot is not a lonesome one. (Discomfort and uncertainty do indeed like comfort.) The tales are not told with bitterness, but more with wonderment and distress, and a certain handwringing. The common thread is that of religious unorthodoxy, indifference, and sometimes outright departure from the faith.

Is it because of where my wife and I live? The northeast is supposed to be liberal territory. Is it the circles in which we move? Are our friends out of the ordinary, far out, away from the mainstream? As one who has the church's interests in his prayers, it would be agreeable for me to believe so. But my contacts, my reading and my researches as a writer do not convince me that our experiences, my wife and mine, are much different from the next Catholic's.

In the concrete, once again:

Look up the article, quite extraordinary, in the Autumn 1986 issue of *The American Scholar* by Heinz R. Kuehn, director of communications for the American College of Surgeons, author of several books, and regular contributor to Catholic and other periodicals. Entitled "Catholic Itinerary," the article was a reflective review of Kuehn's religious pilgrimage in life. It detailed the author's fascinating, indeed exciting religious progression from unformed believer of Jewish-Christian background in the old German federal republic, to Catholic convert in the *neudeutschland* of Adolph Hitler, to Catholic enthusiast in the pre- and post-Vatican II church of American Catholicism—years for Kuehn that were full of apostolic challenges and involvements on both sides of the Atlantic. Kuehn's is a long, moving, nostalgic narrative, one animated by love of church and family. Kuehn and his wife had six children. All six are now young adults, some with families of their own. However, Kuehn remarked with what seemed to me a deep touch of sadness, "None [of the six children] has a particular affection for the church as an institution. Their values and their vision of the world are, more or less consciously, impregnated by the values and visions of Christianity; and since our family is close-knit, they feel at home among Christian traditions and symbols. They respect my wife's and my convictions, and we respect theirs."

John Deedy

Kuehn did not dwell on his children's religious life, but he didn't have to. His comment is understood, for he speaks for and of the current situation in many Catholic families —families where the faith survives in a recognizable, even strong way among the parents, but where it has been reduced to some kind of least common denominator, some merely tangential element in the life of their children, and in some instances less even than that.

Bishop Timothy J. Harrington of the Diocese of Worcester, Massachusetts, not long ago anguished over this phenomenon among families of his ecclesiastical jurisdiction. He writes a weekly column in *The Catholic Free Press*, the Worcester diocesan newspaper, and in one of them wrote about "our young adults,...those 18 to 39 years of age," married and single, people from all walks of life, whose "faith is not active," or "if it is alive,...has been put on a back burner." They need the help, the values, the strength of the church, the Bishop exclaimed, but "their enthusiasm for communion with God in the Eucharist" is lost and "slowly but surely they drift away." "I pray for them. I think about them often."

Of course, well he might. And well might we all, for whatever others might contend, I say that the drift of the younger generations of Catholics from the faith or to the fringes of the church constitutes the church's most urgent problem, definitely the most urgent confronting the American church. Rome rides a hawkish shotgun on the discipline and orthodoxy of the clergy and of women religious who dare to assert themselves. But meanwhile the pews empty of those who are the very guarantors of the church's future. I find it mildly ironic that in the general intercessions that follow the recitation of the Nicene Creed at Mass, the matter of vocations to the religious life is regularly broached, and those in the congregation are asked to petition God for a return to the healthy quotas of old. But how often is the congregation asked to pray Bishop Harrington's prayer for the return or for the restimulation of belief of Catholics 18 to 39 years of age? I've never heard that petition once at Mass. It's as though were the church to have a rebirth of vocations to the religious life all its problems would be solved. Nothing could be further from probability. Armies of priests, nuns and brothers are going to be of limited effectiveness apostically, if so far as membership is concerned the church is reduced to a shell of an organization.

It is not my business to set the church's spiritual and administrative priorities, but it seems to me that the longer the church fails to come to grips with the worry that Bishop Harrington articulates and is praying about, the more trouble it is courting for itself. Some years ago—1978, in fact—the National Conference of Catholic Bishops estimated that there were twelve million non-practicing Catholics among the nation's 68-million unchurched. The leadership of the time announced plans for a major evangelical effort to reclaim them, and maybe pick up some strays in the process. Curiously, the project never got off the ground, and one can only wonder why. Certainly the problem was never solved, at least so far as non-practicing Catholics were concerned. That twelve million 1978 figure, conservative to begin with in all likelihood, is today no doubt a fraction of a much larger whole. I don't see young adults carrying forward an enthusiasm for the church of their birth, at least not as a genre. I seem to see more and more young adults moving towards indifference for the church, and fewer and fewer who are bidding or volunteering for participatory roles in the church's life.

Why this should be is as mysterious as it is perplexing. Among several responses to the Kuehn article in *The American Scholar* was one addressing Kuehn's lament that the glow and excitement of being a Catholic has been lost, that even among its own the church does not stand for as much today as did when the Kuehns were raising their children. The respondent, one Piers Lewis, remarked that Kuehn should not be surprised about that. "People of conscience discovered, in World War II, that they would just have to get along with [the church]," he said, "and they have been doing so ever since, with about the same ratio of success to failure as always." The reference, it developed, was to the role the Catholic Church played vis-a-vis Nazi policy regarding Jews and other so-called undesirable races—Lewis' term—of Europe. Its introduction into a discussion about Kuehn's article is certain to strike some Catholics as tendentious. But whether it is or isn't, it does not begin to account for the astonishing drift of Catholics of the younger generations, particularly young American Catholics, from active participation in the faith. A whole other series of elements are involved, ranging from what the pope calls materialism to a variety of social factors, including, I suppose, Yuppie-ism. Question: Does the young crowd today draw more sustenance from brie cheese and white wine than from the eucharist? God, I pray not.

GOD AND ME

In parochial school years ago we used to pray for the missions and the work of the church in foreign lands, and especially for conversions to the faith. Today I pray for the church in my own land, because I worry for the day when it might be something of a mission church itself—not for lack of a clergy (priests could be imported, in fact already are being imported, from Africa and Asia, where vocations are said to be booming); not for lack of baptized members (baptism, along with a few other sacraments, will survive as a rite of passage, giving the church an impressive head count); not for lack of buildings and institutions (the constructs of the American church are too impressive to disappear quickly or easily). I worry for the future of the American church because I am not certain of the interest, commitment and spiritual durability of the new generations of Catholics; I am not certain of their concern for the church's sacramental and organizational life. And so I pray for it. A paranoid's prayer? Maybe, except at least one bishop publicly shares the same worry.

I should say as I draw to the close of this essay that its writing has not been easy. I feel that I have revealed more of myself here than ever before. It has been a chastening experience in a way, for the assignment has forced me to examine conscience—as in the old days of going to confession. It's always good to examine conscience, even if nothing changes immediately and substantially as a result. I cannot say that the exercise is going to get me back to the confessional box. But at least I understand better my relationship with God, and maybe God appreciates my concerns about his/her church.

John Deedy

Maybe, on the other hand, much of this concern of mine is bumptious. Maybe this church does not need my prayers, and maybe it is presumptuous of me to be praying for it. After all, did not Christ promise that he would be with the church all days, even to the end of the world? So what am I being so nervous about? Point conceded—except, come to think of it, we do pray for the church at every Mass we attend—in the prayer over the gifts: "May the Lord accept the sacrifice at your hands for the praise and glory of his name, for our good, and *for the good of all his church."*

We pray for the church, for obviously we don't know exactly what the promise of Christ to be with his church all days translates to. We don't know, for instance, how much and to what extent the position and strength of the church are guaranteed, or where. Asia and Africa may indeed be the future of the church, as some are predicting. But I live in the United States. My children do. My grandchildren do; if more are born, they will too. For all their sakes, and because their souls and their cultural development are involved, I want the American church to be a strong and determining church for them spiritually and religiously—culturally too, because for me the latter is as important as the two formers.

If that isn't enough to make the American church and its new generations the focus of one's prayer life, then what is? If that mightn't dominate the "God and me" relationship of one's sixty-fourth year, what better focus has one to recommend?

THE GOD OF THE GALAXIES: UNITY AND DIVERSITY

Robert C. Marsh

NO part of Christian doctrine troubles the non-Christian more than the idea of the Trinity. (Indeed, it causes troubles within the Christian community, hence the existence of Unitarians.) Yet the Christian concept of deity demands pluralism. God reveals himself to us in multiple roles, and we respond to each of these manifestations of the divine in a different way. The Father, the Son, the Holy Spirit are each unique, yet bound together in the unity of Godhood. As it was established by Christ's teachings, is now, and ever shall be, these three manifestations of the divine are at once separate and one.

Discussing the relationship of a human individual and God requires us, first, to consider how each of the persons of the Trinity relates to humanity. In brief, I see God the Father as the celestial architect, Aristotle's prime mover, he who writes the laws of the physical sciences. His relation to the individual human life appears to be slight. Our link to the divine is the Son, source of the second covenant. He gave himself to liberate us from sin, to offer us the gift of eternal life as children of God, and we turn to him for our primary link to the Godhead. But there remains the Holy Spirit which permeates all that is truly of God, and through its light we see God's work, God's law, God's presence in our lives.

148

Robert C. Marsh

In antiquity even the wisest man had no real understanding of earthly geography, let alone the structure of the heavens. The Earth was commonly regarded as the center of the cosmos, and the cosmos was a fairly small place. The Greeks, in time, developed the beginnings of scientific astronomy, but this had little effect on religious matters. Accurate, observational astronomy and religion were still at odds with one another in Western Europe during the renaissance.

Twentieth century humanity must view things very differently. We inhabit a beautiful blue planet attached to a yellow dwarf, an insignificant middle aged star in an enormous galaxy. The cosmos appears to have no center. Certainly we cannot consider our place in space to have that importance. "The fundamental error of imagining that human life was fundamentally different from the rest of nature gave rise to many an odd doctrine," writes Timothy Ferris in *Galaxies*. And thus, any proper understanding of God as the celestial architect requires some appreciation of what he designed.

Until the present century, when adequate telescopes and other research devices became available, no one fully grasped the enormity of the cosmos in which we find ourselves. There are 200 billion stars in the galaxy of which we are a part, and there are about a 100 billion major galaxies in the cosmos as we know it. (Three of them are visible to the naked eye.) So if each galaxy averages only 100 billion stars (we shall be modest in our estimates) and there are 100 billion galaxies, this suggests the existence of 10,000 billion stars. If only two per cent of them have planets, we still have 200 billion planetary systems. If only

149

one percent of these have any form of life, life still exists in two billion places in the cosmos. God has a lot to look after.

The rationalist philosophers argued whether the cosmos was finite or infinite and if it had a beginning in time. They were unprepared to do this with authority because the resolution of the question required evidence that humankind did not possess until quite recently, and to try to settle the issue on purely rational grounds produced the follies Immanuel Kant exposed so ruthlessly in his *Critique of Pure Reason.* Kant was a highly competent cosmologist for his day. He sensed the true size of the heavens and the fact that, beyond our galaxy, other galaxies burned bright in the skies.

The attraction of the steady state theory which Fred Hoyle and others advanced so persuasively in the 1950s was that it eliminates the issue of when the cosmos came into being. It is always in change, but in its essential features, it is always the same. And it always had been like that. The regression was infinite. To ask about a beginning was nonsense. This reflects a basic predisposition of mid-century positivism, when the ideal way to get rid of troublesome questions was to try and establish that they were nonsensical.

Aristotle was quite aware of the significance of arguments that presuppose infinite regression. Writing in the fourth century before Christ, he stated that "the material generation of one thing from another cannot go on *ad infinitum* . . . . If there is no first term there is no cause at all." The cosmos of which we are a part appears to be approxi-

mately 18 billion years old. It *did* have a beginning in time:
the event astrophysicists now call the Big Bang. Indeed,
at the risk of seeming factitious, from the standpoint of
infinity, 18 billion years is really not a very long time, or,
putting it differently, it is difficult to imagine that 19 billion
years ago nothing existed at all.

The young Bertrand Russell, as part of his Victorian
religious education, was asked the question, "Who made
me?"

The proper answer was "God made me."

Precocious Bertie then asked "Who made God?" The
vicar did not have an answer and a lifetime of religious
skepticism began. But the answer is suggested by Aristotle.
Any God made by another cause would be lesser than
the cause that made him. Thus the true God made himself.
That has to be an axiom at the start of the argument. God
created himself. Did He exist 19 billion year ago? I am quite
confident he did. He may have existed for quite a long time.

Russell went on to write *Religion and Science,* a book
that has the single virtue of summing up in a concise manner the atittude widely held in the early part of this century that science had in some manner destroyed any
rational foundation for religious belief. I do not think this
was ever true, and I find that it is increasingly recognized
that the primary issues of religious faith and worship cannot be proved or disproved by scientific techniques. The
continuing battles between religion and science appear to
involve both religion and science in fairly primitive, un-
sophisticated form. If the Big Bang theory is true, this has
no effect upon the status of the creation myths in the open-

ing lines of *Genesis*. Creation myths must be studied for what they are. "Creation science" that begins with these myths interpreted literally certainly *is* nonsense, but if we conclude there is no inconsistency between the Big Bang and the cosmos coming into being because of a celestial architect, we are demonstrating that religious men and women can often interpret scientific findings in a manner harmonious with their faith. Russell's social philosophy, one must note, did not depart seriously from basic Christian definitions of the good. He simply had no sympathy for organized religion and wished to develop his ideas from a secular foundation.

The cosmos we know is almost certainly finite—at least in the sense that we cannot see out of it. This is not a problem of instrumentation. In all probability, some time in the middle of the next century when we have an elaborate observatory in space, it will still be apparent that at the edge of things there is a point beyond which we cannot see. The finite limit to the cosmos is not a physical barrier but the point at which all light returns. Light may, theoretically, move in a straight line for an infinite distance, but this would only happen if there were no disturbances due to gravitation. We know that light is bent by gravitational forces, and the cosmos is full of forces of this type, so if the course of light is deflected from a straight line to a curved one, however slightly, sooner or later it will circle in on itself.

If the cosmos is finite, we may wonder about the scope of the divine architect's design. If it was possible that he was at work 19 billion or more years ago, may he not have a hand in another cosmos, or many other cosmic systems, apart from ours, of which we can know nothing? Our cosmos does not extend to the limits of time or the limits of space, but there is no reason to think that the great architect does not work in infinite time and infinite space. It is all his to develop as he wills.

If the Jews were the first to understand monotheism, Aristotle was the first to write systematic theology. The two events are separated by some distance in time. Abraham lived about nineteen centuries before Christ; Aristotle four. But in book Lambda of the *Metaphysics* we have the first and perhaps still most poetic account of God as the celestial architect.

There must be a beginning to events in the heavens, Aristotle says, and that beginning must be the unmoved mover, which exists of necessity. It is good because nothing can happen to it that is contrary to its nature or against its will.

"On such a principle," he writes, "the whole physical universe depends. God's life is a life which is *always* such as the noblest and happiest we can live—and that only briefly while we are examining subjects such as this. . . . Divine thought, being independent of lower faculties, must be thought of what is best in itself, thought that, in the fullest sense, is based on what is best in the fullest sense . . . . If then God is always in a contemplative state of the sort we occasionally achieve, this must excite our wonder; and yet he is in an even better state, which must inspire even greater awe. God must also have life, for the actuality of thought is life [here Aristotle anticipates Descartes' *cogito ergo sum*]. And God *is* that actuality. His essential activity is life most good and eternal. God is therefore a living being, eternal, and most good; to him belong—or rather he is—life and duration, continuous and eternal." Plato decided the finest ruler in human society would be a philosopher king. Aristotle does him one better and entrusts the universe to a philosopher God. I can worship that kind of deity.

One of the fundamental problems in reading the Bible is the interpretation of metaphor. The danger is always that the interpretation will be overly literal and that the meaning will thus be lost. Nowhere, I feel, is this a greater danger than when dealing with the idea of creatures created in the image of God. God is the omnipresent life-affirming force. All living creatures are affirmations of him. His image is the image of life, whether it is here or in some distant galaxy. God sets processes in motion and lets them run to their logical end. More than ninety percent of what is happening in the cosmos is that lifeless matter is moving and changing in accordance with the laws of the physical sciences. Deists look to nature for the proof of the existence of God, as we may as well, but with a different attitude toward what we see and hear. The individual, contemplating the heavens, cannot feel anything less than extreme humility. We want to feel that the author of the cosmos, the celestial architect, knows of our existence and has concern for us as individuals. He has shown this by sending us his son. We sense the tiny specks of life in this enormity of space must be especially precious to him. We may fear his indifference, fear that he thinks of species

Robert C. Marsh

rather than individuals, fear that we are unworthy of his attention. But this is his decision. We have no right to demand his love, demand his attention, but if these things are given to us, we give thanks. And through faith and hope we believe those gifts are real.

The traditional idea of God the Father as the heavenly king, patterned on our idea of world monarchs, is intellectually inappropriate to our time. Religion cannot hope to thrive if it deals with outmoded imagery of this type. God the Father, creator of heaven and earth, must be the God of the cosmos as we know it, and God of the galaxies, the source of order, life, and harmony. Our link to the divine is the Son, our rabbi, the Christ, bringer of the second covenant. His mission was directed to the Jews. Through them the Kingdom of God was to come into being on Earth. After the failure of that mission, entry into the kingdom was offered to the Gentiles. All who would follow Christ's teachings now had opportunity to become sons, or, I think more properly, children of God. This was, of course the work of the apostles, and notably Paul, who, we read, was called to the new task, after the crucifixion, by the voice of the risen Christ.

We can indulge in a certain amount of historic speculation. If we are to develop a theoretical link between the God of Abraham and Aristotle's prime mover, we must set aside the things which are ethnically bound to Jewish or Greek culture and construct a more abstract account of events. Let us surmise that God the celestial architect made the first covenant with the Jews. He was responsible for the emergence of man as a dominant species.

155

GOD AND ME

(Whether this took place by evolution, as I believe it did, or by special creation, is, at this point, irrelevant.) But in time he finds man lawless and self-indulgent. A flood is sent to destroy all but the most virtuous, and from their line grow new people with whom God may deal. Whether this is myth or history or a mixture of the two is not especially important at this point. God's great experiment was whether a creature with free will, when shown the divine law, would consistently, by choice, *live* by that law. The answer seems to be that some will always turn to God and some will turn away from him. God defines his law. He speaks to Abraham, and, centuries later, Moses. But even after the law has been revealed to the people at Sinai, it is not consistently obeyed. Iniquities call for action. At this point God the architect sends his son to fulfill the prophecies, inaugurate the necessary reforms, and bring the Kingdom of God into being.

Is Christ sufficiently human in character to be a convincing intermediary between God and man? In the doctrine of the Trinity, he is God. But in studies such as Michael Grant's *Jesus: An Historical Review of the Gospels*, to which I am intellectually much in debt, the question of his divinity is kept separate from his historical role.

Let us then consider the troublesome man the Romans called Joshua Bar Joseph, born into Jewish society approximately two thousand years ago and destined to change the world. Joshua—or Jesus as we know him—worked within Judism as he discovered it. His mission was to convince his fellow Jews that the prophecies of Isaiah were about to be fulfilled. He reads the lesson in the synagogue

Robert C. Marsh

in Nazareth and says, "Today, in your very hearing, this text has come true," but those who hear him are scandalized. The prophecies were central to the Jewish tradition, but if they were to be fulfilled at all, these events were to take place far in the future. This was presumption in the highest degree. His family turned against him, and he gathered a group of disciples, some of them possible political extremists. Even they often fail to grasp his message, but with them he traveled and taught in Galilee for about two years until the civil authorities regarded him as dangerous and he decided to go elsewhere.

The end of this journey was Jerusalem where the wealthy conservatives who held power in the temple and the Roman city hall gang both regarded him as a threat to the peace. They were not ready for the Kingdom of God. This was the Kingdom of Caesar. Deals had been made. No one was permitted to rock the boat. Jesus was prepared for this. He saw himself now as an alternative form of the Messiah, foretold in Isaiah (Ch. 52/53), not the militant liberator, but the righteous, suffering servant "who bears the sins of the many and by his martyrdom has interceded for their transgressions." His death, on a political charge, does not close the issues he raised, although, to the superficial onlooker, "his life," as Grant puts it, "seemed to have ended in complete failure and disaster." The religious and political establishments were both triumphant.

But what Jesus taught was not forgotten. It was now necessary to take the word to those who were willing to listen and understand and change their lives. There had always been Jews who were prepared to do this. But when

Paul begins to spread the news of Christ's teaching, the Jews are no longer to be regarded as a uniquely chosen people. All who follow the Son of God may become parties to the new covenant which he represents.

In the Roman Catholic Church a more human link to the divine has been seen in the person of the Blessed Virgin Mary, a woman uniquely touched by God, but still mortal. The saints have also played a special role from the beginning as fellow humans with special qualities which bring them God's favor and, through this, a provenance as intermediaries between the human and the divine. I am not opposed to this, but I am not sure it is necessary. Christ is not indifferent to us. He tells his disciples, "I am with you always to the end of time." This is a metaphorical statement in part, but it is not entirely metaphorical. Christ is with us to the degree that we are with him, and that leads to further issues.

Those who knew Jesus saw him as a prophet, a compassionate teacher in the Jewish tradition, conservative in many ways, but not afraid to depart from that tradition and speak boldly for himself when the subject might require it. Historically the prophet and the teacher were replaced by Christ the judge. Look at a medieval French cathedral or Michelangelo's altarpiece in the Sistine Chapel and he is presiding over the last judgment, separating the blessed from the damned. This makes him a more formidable figure. We may pray to him, but the saints and his blessed mother are emotionally more appealing to many.

But who are the blessed? Who are the damned? Fundamentalists may talk of Heaven as a physical place with streets paved with gold, filled with the sound of harps and music in praise of God sung by celestial hosts that put even the Mormon Tabernacle Choir to shame. Can this be taken seriously? Is a Hell of eternal flames any more convincing? Both these elements can be found to some degree in the literature of every Christian church, but the truth, I believe, is more subtle and complex.

Heaven and Hell are states of being, conditions of the spirit. Both can be known, to some degree, in life, just as, in the deepest contemplation, we can, as Aristotle suggests, obtain some glimpse into the mind of the celestial architect. Heaven and Hell are in our minds, our hearts, and Jesus knows the truth of what is there. We cannot deceive him. He judges us by looking within us. It is not a matter of opening the great book in which some enterprising celestial bureaucrat has recorded how many times we failed to attend church or looked with lust upon an airline stewardess. What is important is what is in the center of our being, whether we live by the spirit of the new covenant or not, whether we are prepared to enter into the Kingdom of God here or elsewhere. If we are sincere in our commitment to God's kingdom, our joy in being one with God can be seen. If we are not, we reveal our sorrow in our deeds every day of our lives. Jesus does not keep records. We do. And he knows where to find them.

If his ministry to us ended about 30 A.D., may we speculate what he has been doing since then? The implication in Christian thought is that Jesus rose into heaven and has quietly stayed there, and I find this quite at odds with the character of the man I find represented in the gospels. In the pure joy of speculation, may we not wonder if the Son of God has not visited other worlds where life exists, that he may not be endlessly active going to life forms in their own image with the word of the divine father? His life on Earth was a unique event in our history, probably lasting about 30 years, but he is immortal. Can we be sure we are the first people to whom he spoke? Or the last? There is absolutely no evidence either way, but we can wonder. Surely we are not the only living creatures that deserve to hear the divine word? If we accept that, we can escape from the homocentric universe a primitive science forced the ancients to accept. Even the idea of the universe—the everything—is suspicious to me. We are not sure we know what makes up the everything.

And we can wonder too about life after death. Belief in reincarnation is not a heresy in the Christian faith because there is so little in the Bible that applies. Gautama, the founder of Buddhism, lived approximately 500 years before Jesus, although there is no evidence that his teachings were known to the Jews at the time of Christ. The Buddhist doctrine of rebirth, in which the soul returns in higher (or lower) life forms as a symbol of its spiritual progress (or regression) is not in harmony with Christian teachings, since Christianity does not believe any creature but man to possess a soul.

In one sense, the immortality of all life-forms is assured. The largest part of our bodies, of the plants and animals, is hydrogen which was formed in interstellar space billions of years ago. Its immortality is guaranteed by the laws of physics. But we may take slight consolation that we have in our bodies atoms that probably once were parts of dinosaurs and may, in time, be part of many other living things. We identify ourselves with the center of consciousness, the ego, or, if you prefer, the soul. What of the migration of souls among life-systems in the galaxy, or even between galaxies if the enormous distances can be overcome? I am not concerned with what Gilbert Ryle dismissed as "the spook within" in his *The Concept of Mind*. I think of the soul as a small force field, a dynamic center of energy that has been the source of living processes in an individual. I really am not interested in founding the science fiction school of theology, but I speculate about the soul making the grand tour and, over billions of years, participating in life in many galaxies. Eternity is a long time, after all. Is this contrary to the will of the celestial architect? Why could it not be part of his design in its greatest aspects? The Kingdom of God, surely, is as large as God himself, and God is not Earthbound.

Finally I turn to the subject of God as the Holy Spirit, and here, at last, I can write more fully about the personal element which these essays are supposed to explore.

God for me is primarily the Holy Spirit as expressed by the greatest workings of the human mind. He is the great creator of harmony, not only the music of the spheres, but the concept of peace on Earth through the rule of law. As I see it, all that is true, beautiful, and good reflects the Holy Spirit, for it is through working in harmony with the Holy Spirit the true, the beautiful, and the good come into being. Things of the spirit have no substance and thus can be extended infinitely. We will never run out of truth, any more than we are in danger of running out of faith, hope, or love. Whatever we need is there.

God offers us divine grace, but we need not accept it. We must recognize the fact that this grace is ours, if we wish it. That is the essence of the freedom of our will, for, if we wish, we can reject him—and that is the path to the suffering we may choose to call Hell. But the central element in this process is not the form of our actions but the spirit behind them. It is not simply a matter of doing the right thing. It must be done for the right reason. We can go to church and still reject God. We can walk in the woods, far from any church, and see the trees as his cathedral, and he can be with us as much as in any formal place of worship. What is important is what is in our hearts, our minds. God is infinite in his understanding and his mercy. He asks us to love him and, because of that love, to love our neighbor, whom he also loves, as ourselves. That is the cornerstone of the second covenant. And if we love him, he will not reject us. Whatever passing mortification of the flesh we may be required to endure, his love remains.

I find nothing odd about the possibility that persons who profess no religious faith at all, but spend their lives serving humanity, are, whether they recognize it or not, touched by the Holy Spirit. In short, one can come into harmony with God without seeking to do so, without any knowledge that one has done so—other than a sense of satisfaction with one's achievements. Consider the irreligious Jew who gives hours every day perfecting his skills so he can play the violin as beautifully as possible? If this person is not in some way serving God, who is he serving?

Robert C. Marsh

Without appearing paradoxical, I feel, looking backward, that I have always lived a Christian life, ever aware, in some way, of the presence of the Holy Spirit, even though there were periods when I went for several years without attending a religious service. I went through my positivist stage, during which I lived for a time in the house in the British Cambridge in which Ludwig Wittgenstein had died and, in fact, occupied the room in which he did his final philosophical writing. When I learned that he had requested and received the last rites of the Roman Catholic Church, I took a fresh look at my religious point of view.

One of the things I came to understand was that my attitude toward God could be different from my attitude toward the institution, run by fallible humans like myself, that is his church. To be critical of the church is not necessarily to be critical of God. Not everything that has been done in God's name faithfully represents God's will. The spirit of Christ's teachings has often been forgotten by those professing to represent him. Our approach to sacramental Christianity today should not be colored by historical phenomena such as a Borgia pope and the Spanish Inquisition. Out of these considerations I formulated what, presumably, must be called my mature religious viewpoint in which I could worship Aristotle's philosopher God with conviction and accept Christ's teachings in a more appropriate social and historical context.

The cosmos contains one kind of law—we may call it the laws of physics—which governs whatever happens to material things down to the smallest subatomic particle. We assume these laws are the same at all times and in all

163

places. It also contains what, for the lack of a better term, we can call spiritual harmony. In our thoughts and actions we either join in that harmony or clash with it. The clash, the dissonance, we can call sin, error, immorality. The choice of terms makes little difference. We have put ourselves at odds with the Holy Spirit.

I do not wish to suggest that this is a comprehensive, strictly defined ethical code that God enforces in all places at all times. Moral rules suitable for the entire cosmos would have to be stated in very general terms. Perhaps the basic one is: affirm life. The details must be worked out to fit the specific circumstances. But I do believe that life affirming acts are good, and thus in harmony with the Holy Spirit, while life-threatening things, from going to war to chain smoking, are at odds with the Holy Spirit, do us no good, and destroy harmony.

The central issue between God and man is the problem of evil. In the Jewish tradition the believer is required to live according to the law, and in obedience to the law he finds divine favor. But the fact that he respects the law does not mean that he is spared suffering. Like Job, he may suffer greatly, and still he must submit gladly to the divine will. Many pious Jews, we are told, went to their deaths in the holocaust accepting that it was God's wish that this should be. Their Lord did not betray them when a life of worship ended in the gas chamber. He was with them there, and he knew the meaning and purpose of their death. The Jewish believer is here not far from the tradition of much Eastern mysticism which simply tells us that the things in life which we perceive as good and evil are equally illusory. The metamorphosis of the spirit is real. This is what lifts us to higher levels of enlightenment. From the standpoint of eternity, the pleasures and sufferings of the mortal state are passing moments.

God need not surrender his power and enter a contract with man on the lines that in return for worship and obedience man will be protected against all misfortunes. But the first covenant established a divine law, which man was to honor, and in the second covenant that law was redefined. We must accept the fact that we are tested and tempered by misfortune, as we often are educated by grief. The existence of evil provides us with opportunities to show our strength and prove the sincerity of our convictions.

Consider a world, perhaps not far from us in space, in which God's law was always obeyed in the most scrupulous detail and the believers were rewarded with a life that contained no trouble, no stress, no pain. The central activity of the society would be formal worship. A society of this type would be life-affirming by being God-affirming, showing its dedication to him who is the beginning of all life. But, I think, it would also be a static society. Genius would not thrive there.

Except for a special few, formal worship should not be the central activity in life. A truly life-affirming society, as I see it, is one in which individuals perform significant, even heroic, acts, in which their faith carries them to levels of intensity and dedication in which they worship not passively, but actively, by negotiating a peace treaty or inventing a wonder drug or composing a symphony. These are all acts filled with the power of the Holy Spirit and enriching the divine harmony.

My approach to worship has, I fear, always been rather personal and slightly unorthodox. We worship God when we serve God, and a distinction must therefore be made between formal worship, involving a clergy and a liturgy, and informal worship in which the worshiper is his own priest. This is the most intensely personal form of worship which everyone must perfect for himself, but it may bring the closest feelings of the divine presence.

A problem which I have faced most of my adult life was that I was not certain what my religious affiliation really was. My religious training all came from my mother's family, and it reflected the historical divisions of Northern Ireland that continue to produce unrest today. I was told that there was plausible evidence that my grandfather, Joseph Becket, a member of the Church of Ireland, was descended from St. Thomas of Canterbury (in spite of the variation in spelling the name). Becket is not a saint of the Anglican church. One of my ties to the Roman faith has always been that it honors his martyrdom. I could verify for myself that my grandmother's ancestors, the Mac-Artains, were one of the most ancient and honored Roman Catholic families in County Down. My grandmother became a member of the Episcopal Church when she married my grandfather after they moved to North America, but I think she remained a Roman Catholic at heart, and her favorite son, for whom I was named, went back to the faith of his grandfather for whom my son is named. The practical consequences of this are that I was nominally raised an Episcopalian but that my viewpoint was basically Roman. You could start a fight if you called me a protestant. My first wife was an Episcopalian; my second wife is a Roman Catholic. I serve as a lay reader in St. James Episcopal Cathedral and frequently attend mass with my wife and son at St. Michael's Redemptorist, our Roman Catholic parish church. And I feel perfectly content, perfectly at home in both places.

In earlier periods of my life my dedication to formal worship was linked to a situation I found congenial. In the early 1950s I worshiped at the Church of the Atonement, a high Episcopal church in Chicago, but when I moved to Kansas City, Mo., where the Episcopal Church proved to be quite protestant in its services, I transferred myself to a nearby Roman Catholic Church, St. Francis Xavier, and worshiped happily with the Jesuits during my year in that city. My most rewarding affiliation dates from my Harvard period when I attended the Church of the Advent at the foot of Beacon Hill on the Boston side of the river. The rector, Whitney Hale, represented the finest elements of the high Episcopal Church. I have never felt more at home in a place of worship than I did under his roof.

A basic distinction between the sacramental approach to worship and the services of many protestant churches is that when the sacrament is the center of the service, the priest becomes God's servant. One goes to church to worship God. When the highpoint of the service becomes the sermon, the inspirational thought of some celebrated preacher, the impression is given that many go to church to worship him. I am offended by any church in which the pulpit becomes the altar, telling us clearly that Dr. So-And-So's message is the important thing. We will always need new prophets and teachers, but they must be part of the tradition of prophecy and teaching that begins with the Old Testament. We are renewed by the presence of Christ, which is the focal point of the service in both the Episcopal and Roman Catholic churches.

As we read of Christ's miracles we frequently encounter a Jewish tradition that ascribes sickness to either the possession by demons or the body processes being impaired by sin. Demons are outside the scope of scientific medicine. Physical illness caused in whole or part by mental states is, on the other hand, a familiar part of modern medical practice.

I refuse to think of sickness as punishment for sin. God does not work this way. I can, however, see certain sickness in close relation to certain ways of life that appear to me to be out of harmony with the Holy Spirit. If you are an alcoholic, a destructive state that is a denial of life, it is no surprise that your liver might fail and kill you. If you smoke too much you play havoc with your lungs. Drugs take their toll. AIDS seems less a condemnation of homosexuality than sexual promiscuity, which has always been life-threatening. Increasingly we encounter the idea that the frequency of sexual experiences is more important than their character or quality. But the greatest meaning of sexuality is found when it acquires a spiritual dimension, when two persons genuinely touch one another's hearts. The sad

Robert C. Marsh

truth is that orgasms are relatively easy to achieve but that intimacy requires a great deal of effort. We must learn to give ourselves. The person who forms stable relationships is far less likely to become infected with AIDS. God is not sending a plague to punish evildoers. The evil here we generate ourselves. We violate the harmony.

What then of the good, devout man or woman who after years of Christian life is found to have a destructive disease? First, we are aware of the mortality of the flesh. It was never suggested that the devout Christian should be spared death. Secondly, we must not look upon this sickness as a judgment, although it may be a final test of our faith and moral principles. It is a temporary thing, part of the rite of passage from this life to the life of the world to come. God has not abandoned us, and we have no justification to abandon him. We must try to bear our afflictions with dignity. They will pass.

Socrates, addressing his justices, says: "Be of good cheer about death, and know of a certainty, that no evil can happen to a good man, either in life or after death."

What do these words mean? I have lived with them through my adult life, and for me the message is simple. If there is goodness in our hearts, it will sustain us through any trial. True evil is not that we become ill, or face bankruptcy, or lose a beloved friend. These are painful events. We may well grieve for them, but we will survive and we will still be good. *True evil is the loss of virtue in ourselves.*

The dominant moral philosophy today is what I would call simple-minded hedonism—simple-minded because the basic premises have been accepted without any serious examination. Rarely in history has there been a more dramatic contrast between the traditional religious life of celibacy and poverty dedicated to the Holy Spirit and the good as it is commonly defined in the world at large. There is almost no serious debate over ethics going on in philosophy faculties and, if these issues are raised, the public, even the university community, ignores what is being said. It is characteristic that for some years the most fashionable 20th century philosopher in many university departments was Wittgenstein who avoided problems of value. If philosophers duck these questions, the crackpots take over. Socrates should be there to debunk the sophists, but he is not, and he has been missed. They are telling us that if you have lots of money, lots of sex, lots of fun, you have it made. I am no puritan. Money, sex, and fun all have a place in life. But so does moral excellence, and that is where you find the Holy Spirit.

If a man's happiness depends on things external to himself, a luxurious home, a beautiful mistress, lavish entertainment, he may well lose all these things and his happiness with them. They will not console him on his death bed if within his heart he is empty. This has been part of the wisdom of the race since antiquity. But if the source of his happiness is his inner goodness, his harmony with God, nothing can take this from him. He can face martyrdom if necessary, knowing it to be only an apparent evil.

Christ's kingdom, as he told us, is *not* of this world. Christ's goodness is *not* made up of worldly things. Neiman Marcus has a lot of fancy items for sale, but serenity is not

Robert C. Marsh

one of them. That we must produce for ourselves. The Holy
Spirit enters us when we open our hearts and minds and
let him enter. He is always there. No appointment is required.

Christ was critical of the rich because he felt that they
were obsessed by their possessions and this stood in the way
of their entry into the Kingdom of God. The poor would
not have this problem. There is no reason why a rich person must become a slave to riches, but it happens. And
this slavery is as demeaning as any other. It halts the growth
of the spirit and so denies life.

My mentor at Harvard, Robert Ulich, insisted that all
values must have transcendental authority, otherwise they
would be corrupted, trivialized, and ignored. But we are
living in a secular age. The idea that all value comes from
God cannot carry weight with the irreligious, and the de-
cay of values which Ulich feared is well advanced.

A more important issue is that God, as a source of value,
is limited to issues of ethics and law. God has established
standards of religious conduct. He has defined basic principles of law that apply in both the civic and religious jur-
isdictions, and he has given us the foundations of a moral
code that establishes standards for our conduct toward one
another. But he has not, with any comparable authority
or precision, defined the beautiful in art or the sublime
in poetry. These important elements of our lives we have
always been obliged to evaluate for ourselves. The medieval
builder, inspired by his faith, produced miraculous works
such as Chartres Cathedral, but God gives us no standards
for architectural criticism. These are the work of men. As

171

a critic of the arts, I was unsympathetic to Ulich's point of view because I was obliged to make evaluations on the basis of the qualities I discovered within the artistic experience. If evaluation of this type could be made effectively without any transcendental authority, could not standards of morals and law be established in the same manner? And, as Russell suggested, such standards might carry weight with the religious and the irreligious alike.

As I wrote earlier, God's moral laws for the cosmos as a whole, if they deserve to be called such, must, as I see it, take very general form: affirm life processes. Respect the great harmony of the system. Moreover we must recognize that God as the celestial architect sees the system, not the individual. How, one may ask, can we talk so about the affirmation of life when life is constantly being destroyed? The biological food chain calls for plants to be eaten by herbivores and herbivores to be eaten by carnivores who, in turn, are eaten by other living things, not the least of them bacteria. But a well balanced, smoothly functioning food chain is a magnificent affirmation of life, and if it is working well a vast number of life forms flourish with security. It is not an evil, life-destructive act when a cougar eats a rabbit. They were made for each other. If a certain number of rabbits were not eaten, they would multiply beyond their food supply (a growing rabbit eats something like a third of its weight every day) and die of starvation. The death of the individual rabbit is an inconsequential event, so long as the species can go on.

We must sense the harmony of God's grand design and place ourselves in harmony with it. His great creations are filled with beauty and the sublime, but these qualities are expressed in an incredible variety of forms. This is the clue to the divine esthetic.

In this essay I have said relatively few specific things about love because, as I see it, love is the *cantus firmus* of the entire discussion. If God did not love us we would not exist. If God had not continued to love humankind, despite our transgressions, there would have been no second covenant. Our hope springs from his renewed affirmation of his love. God is harmony and peace and the prime source of harmony and peace is love. Our faith is simply an affirmation of our enduring love of God. The affirmation of life is the affirmation of love. Love is the underlying meaning of it all.

The seven deadly sins—there are really more than seven—are linked by the denial of love, placing the gratification of the ego before any obligation to God or another person. To deny love is to reject God. To put the love of self before the love of God is to choose Hell, to spend a lifetime, if not an eternity, trapped in the pitiful limitations of one's petty desires, rejecting the fullness and richness of life.

There have been many lists of virtues written through the centuries. My favorite, at the moment, are The Ten Perfections of Buddhism. It is a prayer I say almost daily.

"I shall seek to develop the perfection of generosity, virtue, doing without, wisdom, energy, forbearance, truthfulness, resolution, love, serenity."

Any good Christian can desire these things as much as a good Buddhist, for they define our common humanity at its best. They are fully consistent with the teachings of Christ. They show us how the Holy Spirit can best work through us to bring the Kingdom of God to pass.

And what, as the 21st Century beckons us, is the Kingdom of God in our world? It is, I think, a world free of war or the threat of war, a world in which all nations work together for the common good, a world in which social and political justice rule, in which every individual has an opportunity to make the most of his abilities, in which the best that humanity has achieved becomes the foundation for a new civilization that encompasses the entire Earth. To create such a civilization would be a magnificent achievement for humanity because it represents a victory over the greatest adversity, if not the conquest of Satan, the conquest of the evil within ourselves. And what can that civilization do that no other has achieved? It can reach out to the stars.

THE GIFT

Maureen Daly

ANY comments of mine about "God and me" will have
to be made without conclusions, finality or pithy wisdom since ours has been a rocky, on-going relationship,
sometimes on, sometimes off, that has yet to submit to
definition or even coherent description.

I know more about myself and my relationship with God
by looking backward, rather than forward, by judging
what I *did do* and think and hope in the past in times of
love, deep need or terrible crisis, not what I *shall do* in
the future in those years which Rebecca West describes as
"the grey great oxen plodding on."

At one point in life, some three decades ago, I asked and
received sustenance in a grave illness situation in which
I believed our small daughter was dying. I wrote of this
experience then in story form; it was titled "The Gift" when
printed in a national magazine, but what is recounted here
is truth. I asked the editor of this book to include it as an
open and perhaps naive account of how God and I spent
our time together a few years ago on the small Spanish
Island of Ibiza, in the Mediterrean Sea, far off the Western
Iberian coast. The story goes this way:

* * *

We'd been on the little Spanish island just one day when
Megan became ill. At first she was only fretful, but by the

time the sun went down at ten o'clock that night she was hot and listless. Even without a thermometer, I could tell her temperature was dangerously high.

The evening before, our first in the village, we had unpacked our luggage and then walked down the main street to the cafe in the square. We'd come as tourists to this little island of Ibiza, which was an overnight boat trip from Barcelona, and had taken rooms in Santa Eulalia del Rio, a village of a few dozen houses overlooking the Mediterranean. In the daytime it was bright and windswept; in the early evening it was a static backdrop done in murky pastels.

Before leaving for the cafe, Bill had changed into an old sports shirt and I wore a cotton sun dress and sandals; but in this poor village we were still conspicuously American.

The few tables at the cafe were crowded with village men, sipping absinthe and strong black coffee. No one really spoke to us, but the men nodded to Bill and there was only a small circle of silence around us as we ordered black coffee. Behind the big coffee machine hung an old picture of Franco, faded with steam. It was almost eleven when the last man went home and the cafe owner closed up by unscrewing the single bulb in a hanging socket. When we went back down the main street to our rooms, every light in the village was out, and we had to follow the cart ruts to stay on the dusty roads.

The next morning after breakfast, Megan and I went for a walk in the village, stepping around the flat baskets of peppers, onions, potatoes and figs laid out for sale along the narrow pavements. Straw hats were our first purchases, for even before ten in the morning the sun was intense and the white dust of the street was dazzling.

Megan and I walked as fast as a four-year-old can walk, but her pace put me on a defenselessly intimate basis with the women we passed. They went quietly on with their work, neither hostile nor shy, but almost as if we were not there at all. The main street of the village was no more than a hundred yards long, but it took only half that distance for the women to see that I was an intruder, a stranger who had come only to look.

My walking with a child didn't change their attitude toward me; there was no nodding or smiling, not even on the common bond of motherhood. Suddenly I knew why. Megan was sturdy, almost embarrassingly so, next to the dark-eyed, thin-legged little children playing in the street. Her legs had a firm, solid look and her hair was thick and shiny, without the tiny bare patches that marked some of the children's heads. Her actions seemed almost bold when she tried to shake hands with a little boy who had been staring at us, but then turned and ran crying back to his mother. And his mother didn't smile at me.

These villagers were here to live and die—dependent on the sea, a few green crops and fruit trees and the matted brown sheep that browsed on the hills. They had no time to walk with their children in the sun in the morning.

Later Megan and I sat at a table outside the cafe, watching the water. We sat for a long time over two bottles of lemonade, feeling sleepy in the sun; and still later, when

Megan first began to feel ill, I remembered with worry that the metal caps on the lemonade bottles had been rimmed with rust.

Our rooms were in one of the few two-story houses in the village, cool in the daytime, damply warm and stuffy at night. After I had put Megan to bed that evening, Bill and I sat by the window to get air. Below us, the village was black and silent; Bill's cigarette, as he drew on it, made only a faint, tiny glow in the room. Every half-hour or so we tiptoed in to put damp cloths on Megan's forehead and to be sure she was covered. But she slept almost too soundly, breathing almost imperceptibly, quiet and hot beneath the thin blanket.

It was a long night. It seemed, in the darkness, that something big had gone wrong; we had moved too far against some indefinite but disapproving force. At eleven o'clock at night in this Spanish village, with wavering electricity, no car, no telephone and no friends, it was as though we had slipped back into the Middle Ages.

At home in New York, the night would have been just a short, familiar period until morning. There the thermometer and extra blanket were in the cupboard; the doctor's telephone number was written on the wall next to the telephone. But here, without those props, I was another person. There was not, as I had always expected, some emergency mother-wisdom to draw on. There was nothing. Somewhere in my life, unconsciously or not, I had allowed a faith in panaceas like penicillin to replace religious faith; that night I had neither to depend on.

Bill and I went carefully over everything the child had

done in the last few days. Most of the time at Santa Eulalia del Rio, she has just walked round and round the garden of the house, feeding the little chickens and chasing the big roosters. But, of course, there were the flies, and the dogs she patted in the town, and the bunch of green grapes an old woman had given her when we got off the boat, and the endless strange fish, figs and fried octopus we had all eaten, and the milk I couldn't get anyone to boil, and the drinking water, and the endless beating sun.

We went to bed finally, when there seemed nothing left to talk about.

About five o'clock the morning began to come alive with sounds.

The noise of the sea came more clearly; the trees brushing against the closed, shuttered windows moved with a new breeze. In the garden below, the little chickens woke and began scratching and peeping to be fed. By six, Bill was down in the village looking for a man with a donkey cart who would take him the seven miles across the island to look for a doctor.

Even in our room, I could hear the waking sounds of the village. In a few short hours, the strangeness of the place and the fear of illness had made me acutely conscious of the pattern of living here. At the first moment the sun began to shine, even in its thin morning brightness, the whole town was rushing to do its business and get back into the shadows before the inevitable, unrelenting heat filled the day.

The maid of the house, a sixteen-year-old with a single black plait hanging between her shoulders, brought a tray with cold coffee, a jug of steaming milk, some bread, butter and a saucer of sugar. The bread was cut from a big loaf, musty and a little hard, and the butter was soft and faintly rancid. But I knew there was no point in asking for better food; it was the best to be had in the village. I mixed some of the coffee with hot milk and sugar and spooned a little into Megan's mouth when she waked. Then she drank the whole cup thirstily and seemed well enough, except for the heat of her skin and her listlessness. "Where's Raggy?" she asked in a small voice.

The doll had slipped under the bed during the night and I had to go down on my hands and knees to get it. There seemed something symbolic that morning about the ragged doll with its painted grin, still looking as insolent as when I'd bought it for Megan's third birthday.

It was ten o'clock before the doctor came. Bill and he arrived together in a rattling taxi from the other side of the island. The doctor was a tall, thin man, with gray hair cropped close to his head. Megan's temperature was 104, her throat was inflamed and she barely opened her eyes when he examined her. Since we couldn't speak enough Spanish, Bill explained to the doctor in halting French that she had never before been ill.

The doctor was thoughtful and grave. There was a serious infection of the body, he said. He wasn't sure what. He could not come to see her tomorrow, but he would be back the day after, late in the afternoon. In the meantime, one of the nuns of the village would come to give her penicillin. There was a nursing order on Santa Eulalia, with four sisters to care for about seven thousand people scattered throughout the area. The order were all peasant women, he explained, women of the island. He would stop at the convent on his way back to the other side of Ibiza. He had no telephone, but if the child became worse, Sister Jose would know how to get word to him.

Megan was sleeping heavily when the little nun arrived. Bill and I were watching from the bedroom window when she came trudging up the stony, dusty road to the house, holding up her long skirts, already grayed and heavy with dust. Though it was more than an hour till noontime, the heat had stilled every noise in the village. The children had gone into the dark doorways to play and even the dusty chickens were huddled in the scattered shadows around the yard.

We heard the little nun walking across the dry grass to the back door and a few moments later there was a tap on our bedroom door. I woke Megan gently, to tell her someone was there.

We opened the shutters enough to let in the light without heat, and both Megan and I saw Sister Jose clearly for the first time. She was short, more like a tall child, and slight, even in the folds of her black nun's habit. Her face was pale and smooth, but her hands had a rough, outdoor look, as if she had worked long hours in the garden. Her capable fingers and short nails were scrubbed clean. It was her eyes that gave her that strange, doll-like look—round, brown and very bright. On her breast was pinned a starched circle of white cloth with a lumpy red cross embroidered on it. In one hand was a small black leather bag; the other hand was hidden in the folds of her long skirt.

She smiled at Megan, her twinkling eyes giving her an oddly childish look. As she walked toward the bed, she pulled her hand from the folds of her skirt. There was a tiny baby chick, peeping loudly, stretching its skinny neck. Megan never moved, but she gave a little smile of happiness and whispered, "Mine!"

Very gently, the nun put the chicken on the bed, where it squeaked and toppled among the folds of the blanket. Sister Jose said nothing to either parent—except with her quick smile.

As Megan's eyes followed the chicken, the nun arranged her equipment on a table, wiping her fingers with alcohol, setting up a tiny spirit lamp to sterilize the needle and putting out the little bottle of penicillin. Her movements were quick and professional. A few moments later, I held Megan over my knee while the nun pinched the little hip for the first injection.

Megan gave a squeal of indignation, surprised and angry at being hurt, but in a moment she was lying back on the pillow in contented weariness, the chicken cupped in one hand. By the time the nun had packed her bag and tucked the chick back in the folds of her habit, the child had dropped back to sleep. The whole process had taken less than ten minutes.

By eleven that night Megan had had four injections. Each time the nun had stopped to pick up a little chick in the yard, holding it hidden as she came into the room, her shiny eyes always smiling first at Megan, with just a quick glance for me. Never once did she say a word to us, but set the chick gently on the bed, her silence and the strange, childish excitement she brought with her riveting the invalid's attention to the bird.

For a few moments it was like two children playing, and when the woman turned to light her spirit lamp and get the needle ready, she conferred on Megan her personal excitement and sense of mystery. Never once did the child show fear when the nun came into the room. Never once did she seem to suspect that the sister-nurse brought with her anything but a young chick. But by the fifth shot, wearied with fever, Megan had begun to whimper, even in her sleep.

While the lamp flickered, the nun explained to me in whispered Spanish and special gestures that she would spend the night with us, to give penicillin every three hours. The child and I might share the narrow bed; she would sit up in the big wooden armchair.

Sometime during those long, hot hours I dropped off to sleep. It was about half-past twelve when I woke with that curious nightmare feeling that someone had just spoken aloud. But Megan was sleeping and the nun was sitting upright in her chair. There was no sound in the room except the faint click of her rosary beads as she pulled them through her fingers. There was an alertness about her posture and the evenness of her breathing that showed she had not dozed at all. I was afraid to move, for fear Megan would wake up, so I lay watching the nun in the darkness.

Somehow, Sister Jose sensed I was awake and turned toward me. She raised one hand in a little wave.

Just before one o'clock she got up from her chair, and, in a moment, I saw her pale round face lighted by the tiny blue flame of the spirit lamp. Twice more that night we got up together to give Megan her injections. Just after seven o'clock, the woman took the child's temperature, packed the black bag and went off down the hill to Mass at the village church. At ten, having made her round of patients in the village, both nun and chick were back at our bedroom door.

During a part of the day, Bill sat in the sickroom and I wandered around the hot, sunny garden. Promptly, on every third hour, Sister Jose came up the hills, surrounded by a little cloud of dust. Never once did she look tired, never once did she forget to scoop up a tiny chicken from the flock scratching among the bright geraniums in the back garden. With not a word to understand between us, we had become close friends.

Our second night together was a little more tense, a little more restless than the first, since Megan seemed no better and her fever had been high for well over forty hours. Just before dark, I put cold cream on the child's fever-blistered mouth and sponged the palms of her hands with cologne to cool them. She never even woke when I touched her.

During the night the wind was restless and once, near morning, a little lizard I had seen on the ceiling during the day fell to the floor with a sudden, final flop. I remember thinking that I must be careful to shake my shoes before putting them on the next day. Sister Jose, awake the whole night, paced off the hours with her rosary, her little eyes as bright at midnight as they had been at noon.

Megan's fever broke suddenly, just after sunrise, and

about an hour after her sixteenth injection of penicillin. I lay beside her, feeling her body glued to mine in the heat, and the fever ebbed away so quickly that at first I couldn't be sure it had happened at all. Sister Jose came with the thermometer and put it into the sleeping child's mouth. The temperature was just a little above normal.

Tiptoeing, the nun threw open the shutters to let in the fresh morning air, and then turned to tuck the cotton blankets under Megan's chin. After the two days and two nights without sleep, taking care of us and the sick people of the village, she still looked as neat and unharried as when we first saw her.

Quickly, deftly, she packed the black bag, wrapping the penicillin bottles and needles in a small white cloth. I knew by her haste she was trying to make the seven o'clock Mass. With a last flurry of starched cloth she bent over and kissed Megan on the forehead, then turned to me with a small bow and put out her hand. I held it and said in hurried, make-shift Spanish, afraid she might rush away, "Thank you, thank you, I am grateful. Will you tell me, please, what I owe you, Sister Jose?"

The last words had to be said slowly, accompanied by those curiously vulgar gestures of counting out money.

Her face grew sober. "Ah, I understand," she said. Then she paused. "I must ask you," she whispered sadly, "for eighty-two *pesetas* for the penicillin and for my days. We need money for our work." And then, with her quick smile, she added, "But my nights belong to God—and gladly I give them to you."

A few moments later there was nothing left in the room

GOD AND ME

to show she had been there—except Megan sleeping peacefully, the blanket tucked under her chin, one small hand outstretched and cupped, as if a tiny chick snuggled there.

I didn't even go to the window to watch Sister Jose hurry down the hill in the morning dust. I could hear the church bells from the village and the steady wash, wash of the sea, so constant that it seemed only another kind of silence, and I knew I should hear those sounds again and again, any time in my life I wanted to remember.

We had had only four short years together and for a long part of those years, I had wondered to myself what to tell my child about God. I still didn't know for sure. But I knew that morning I could begin by telling her about the little nun.

* * *

A number of years later, Megan—out of college, married, a career-mother—mentioned to me one day that she had told her children, two little boys, about the Spanish nun, the baby chick and how both had cured her fever.

"Not as I remembered it," she explained, "because it's just a kind of dream to me, but as you told me about it."

"I'm not sure they understood," she went on. "The idea of holding a baby chick was entrancing to them but they couldn't quite understand about the nun. And very few children get penicillin these days. I'll tell them again when they're older. I want them to know about it."

Her sons, Antonio and Nicholas Shaw, were four years old and just under three when, one night in winter, their mother died. Megan never had time to retell them the story of Sister Jose and her gift on the island of Ibiza.

It happened quickly. Megan called me late one afternoon from her home in Glendale, California. Her husband, Richard Shaw, was with her. "You'd better come up, Mo," she said. "I just heard from the doctor about the biopsy. That little lump on my clavicle? It's malignant."

Her case was considered particularly poignant (and not unusual) because her father, the good, patient, loving Bill who had waited out her fever in that bedroom in Ibiza, had died of cancer just a few months before. Megan had mourned deeply for the big, six-foot-four shadow of love that no longer fell across her life. Her defenses, her immunity systems were down, fatally down.

Our prayers and hopes kept pace with the conventional treatments of radiation and chemotherapy for only six months. It was on New Year's Eve that Megan McGivern Shaw died in a Los Angeles hospital, just as the bells of the churches were ringing out over the city, welcoming a new year or mourning one gone by. She was a long way from her last crisis on the little island of Ibiza.

Her husband was with her. I was not. "Whatever you do, Mo," she said as part of her last concerned, loving instructions, "remember that Richard can't do everything."

I was awake and praying as those bells rang, watching over Megan's little boys at home and asleep in their cribs.

Richard, stunned, loving and a pragmatist, had asked her doctors how Megan was to die. He had been told, since the cancer was in her lungs, that she would likely weaken until she suffered a spasm of coughing so severe, so rending to the body that the heart could not survive the torment. It would stop.

I could not accept that graceless, suffering end for someone who had always been a thing of beauty.

From early dusk, when the boys fell asleep, until I got the final phone call from the hospital and Richard that New Year's dawn, I barraged my own God with a special *mantra. "It does not have to be this way."*

I was repetitive, strong, insistent, unrelenting, not pleading but going through a kind of spiritual hand-wrestling to demand what I felt Megan must have. I was not a humble supplicant. I pulled rank, insisted on the privileges of senority. It was now between God and me, a communication to the death. I stood up for my child, I guarded her through that night and I was not turned aside.

Megan did not cough once during those long hours and she was holding Richard's hand, face peaceful, eyes closed, when the morning shift nurse woke him to tell him Mrs. Shaw was dead.

Antonio and Nicholas Shaw are a little older now—just a little older—and they spend a lot of time with me. They will be down for a visit tomorrow. As always, I have things to show them, things to tell them.

For this visit I saved a clipping to read them called "Fascinating Facts about Felines." They love animals and have a cat named Snowball. Together we planted a small garden at my house around the base of a *palo verde* tree. In the mild winter of the California desert, they are going to be able to pick tomatoes for our Christmas salad. Their father loves tomatoes.

Maureen Daly

In one bedroom we keep an old wind-up music box that plays *La Vie en Rose* (at bedtime) and they like to remember when their mother played it for them. Sometimes they get out of bed in their pajamas and dance. If they are willing to put on slippers and sweaters, they can sit out in the back garden for a while and try to name the stars. They both can write their names in block letters.

Once we went for a long walk in the nearby desert. The sky was so blue that day that the jagged brown mountains looked like something cut out and pasted on a kindergarten window. Antonio pointed and shouted, "There's a big-horn sheep!" It was a ram standing so high and far away on a distant crest that its great, muscled body and curved horns were like a perfect, magic miniature etched on the horizon. Antonio kept pointing till his brother saw it, too.

I doubt if I shall ever tell the Shaw brothers about Sister Jose and the island of Ibiza and their four-year old mother and the nights that belonged to God. That should have been Megan's story.

But there are so many other ways of saying the same thing. Every time they come to visit me now, the boys ask to go walking in the desert. They are determined to see the great big-horn sheep again and I keep telling them they will. "Keep looking," I say to Megan's children. "Keep looking and you'll see it. It's all out there."

I feel certain that some day those boys will tell their little ones about that great, big-horned sheep. And somewhere deep in their psyches, as faint as the song from the music box, they may remember a young mother and a strange, faraway story about a nun and a small chick. And it will not make them unhappy to wish they might have heard it again.

As I said in my first few lines about "God and me," I am a wandering soul, thoughtful, emotional, critical and, in view of what has happened in recent years, strangely—even pathetically—hopeful.

I have not always gotten what I asked for from God and I certainly never asked for much of what I get. We have had an on-going relationship with periods of doubt, ambivalence, euphoria and sometimes unquestioning trust.

It's been an inter-dependency pattern of a lifetime. I do not seem to live for God, but I do not live without him. My demands, my beliefs, will not allow that.

We made a mutual bargain some months ago, God and I, and we are working on it now. I know I shall never break my word on our agreement and I expect him to observe and honor His implicit promises.

The pact was made only moments after those fateful bells of New Year's Eve rang out and a young woman, for the first time in her short, brilliant life, could no longer hear them.

For all the time I am part of this earth, I vowed that night, I shall love, care for and find joy for Megan's sons. I expect God, with his limitless quota of eternity, to do no less for my child.

ALL THE FULLNESS OF GOD

Barbara Doherty, S.P.

IN MY book, *I Am what I Do*, I outlined in pictures and words the experiences people have of God. I have never found it necessary to change those ideas too radically because the experiences people have of the Divine are similar through centuries and cultures. Now I am asked not to write in general terms about humanity's experiences of God but to write about God and me. Because our experiences of God evolve and because God does not abandon us, what I write this moment is in a sacred process. What I write about God and me in another year or in a different set of life circumstances will have some changes in it. I hope these will reflect new wisdom and depths gained.

God is in the warp and the woof of my human existence. I believe that that aspect of Holy Mystery, which we call the Holy Spirit, is radically imminent to my personal history and to the corporate history of all people. Yet, I find myself strangely reluctant to put down in black and white the experiences I know of the divine activity which undergirds my life. There is something private about these experiences. They tell of holy ground deep within to which others usually have no access. In addition, it is a struggle to bring articulation to what is inarticulate. Nonetheless, *God and Me* is the name of the task at hand. One can only trust that to share an experience so personal and so full of nuances and uncertainties may serve one's companions as, with difficulty and trepidation, we make our journey through the few years we inhabit the planet earth in human form. The experience which I define in *I Am What I Do* as the contemplative experience of God is the one that, for many years, I have known, grappled with, misunderstood and welcomed. It will be that contemplative journey to which I attempt to put a few halting words, words that even this extrovert hesitates to make public.

Naturally, my early experiences of God were similar to many other young persons' experiences of God. More than likely, the way in which we knew parental presence had everything to do with the way we felt or knew godly presence. A great amount of healing and confirming, through people and events experienced as godly messengers, is necessary for someone whose parental memories are tragic and tangled. For those of us for whom home and parenting had great amounts of faith, stability and security, the godly presence was obviously similar.

I am an oldest child and an eldest grandchild. The circle of benevolence around my early years was extended from parents, grandparents, aunts and uncles. My childhood was normal though now I realize that a happy, secure childhood may be abnormal given the numbers of pathetic, pain-filled family situations. The Doherty family fitted the Catholic portrait of the Chicago church of the 40's. We went to Mass every day, said the rosary together and did all the Catholic things expected of us. I don't presently recall feeling oppressed about it. I am a ghetto Catholic; I think I probably thought that even the neighborhood dogs were Catholics. Anyone who was not a Catholic could expect a cogent argument from my father—Lord have mercy on him—which clearly and completely showed them the error of their religious choices.

God was a given. All the holy of heaven and all the meaning structures clarifying earthly existence were part of the air I breathed. I know now that the security, direction and purposes of my early years set me on a determined course that has been honed and refined by life's chastenings but which has become more firmly established explanations of reality within me through ensuing years.

For readers who experience only ambiguity, darkness and struggle, please know that security/direction/purpose do not eliminate or very often even enlighten ambiguity/darkness/struggle. It is these varied stances balanced within me, however, that I name the Poises of the Infinite or the Faces of God before and within which I live out my Catholic journey.

In adolescence, given proper parenting, the distance between parent and child is overcome and comradeship can develop. Similarly the distance between God and us begins to be overcome as we move into adolescence. God is nearer, walks beside us and informs our decisions. As an adolescent, belief in God began to demand of me. I'm not too certain how this difference came about, but I knew that behaviors like fighting with my middle sister were not what a Christian ought to be doing. I'm certain that if anyone polled my sister, she would testify that she never experienced anything of my gathering Christian resolve; however, there was a new dimension of godliness within me, more than likely occasioned by religion classes and Catholic clubs which urged Christlike behavior. I have some instinct that I was probably obnoxiously arrogant about the whole development (oldest children are frequently capable of egregious self-righteousness), but my religious changes were predictable given the circumstances of family, school and Catholic action groups which filled my days. A boyfriend, somewhat older and wiser, urged me away from college frolics and toward concern for the neighbor met at Friendship House, the Little Sisters of the Poor or on Skid Row. Thus the godly was connected early on in my mind with what today is called praxis. In hindsight I can identify these internal awakenings with a growth to personal faith, mission and purpose. Current sociologists (cf. *Habits of the Heart*, ed. Bellah *et al.*) inveigh against the purposeless lives of the young who lack any dimension of vocation toward particular ways to live. They accuse us older citizens of neglecting to hand on a sense of commitment to bettering our world. I am thankful these many years later for the sturdy purposes that, by a particular Providence, designed my psyche.

Of coure many pathways led me from that adolescence to the place I am as I write this essay—a few days before my 56th birthday. God and I have been at many junctures and will be at lots more. Of that, I am certain. I've done a lot of things, met a lot of people, traveled the world over, gotten a Ph.D., become a proper feminist, taken on many responsible jobs including the presidency of a venerable women's college, and certainly through it all I have been led step by step to the religious posture before God which I know today.

Barbara Doherty

The word "led" is significant. It suggests a mentality far from the "do-it-yourself" Catholicism of my early years. Somewhere in my history the polarities of faith and works (Catholics reflecting the latter) became integrated within me—again, a godly doing—and being led, brought or sometimes "dragged" is a process to which I testify. I am who I am because God has brought me to this place. I have been enlightened, knocked down, healed, strengthened and challenged through 56 years—all God's doing coupled with those wonderful secondary casuality persons and events that consistently channel the Divine into my life. Even when I have been unwilling to be reached, persons and events have broken through my reserves to push to the new understanding and to awaken to the new possibility.

I know these changes only in hindsight. My faith assessment of the divine actions in the present moment is usually oblivious, to state the situation mildly. With hindsight I see reasons, movement and growth. In the present I kick and scream against the goad with words like "stupid," "frustrating," and "preposterous." But when all the pieces fall into place weeks, months or even years later, new depths have been sounded and new dimensions of the godly in my human history have been reached.

Astute readers, used to dealing with religious language, have already calculated and measured the "God and Me" of this author, for my language reveals that for a very long time there has been no experience of a "God and Me." This might register with some people as fearful or suspect. Those whose religious language describes God as a faithful friend who sometimes visits and who is sometimes absent are regarded with awe by me because I do not have and have not had for as long as I can recall, God-experiences which I can speak about with language that suggests a thou and a me and the relation between. I resolved this circumstance for myself in my book on contemplation, that is, at least I resolved it theoretically. Living out experiences of "God within life," or being able to recognize any godly dimension in my days is quite another matter.

I have listened to people talk about God walking with them. Usually I hear their words as if they describe an "Invisible-Harvey-the-Rabbit" companion to their days. I have envied their assurance; most often I have questioned it and wondered whether it is merely language that allows them the luxury of a perceptible God while I wander around in a darkness, frequently calling out, "Is there anyone out there?" And as I get older, the question seems to focus on: "Shall there be a You when I die?"

Unfortunately or fortunately, the contemplative experience of God which I have taken pains to elaborate, is not an experience of companionship. In fact, it is not a relational experience at all. I have struggled with the word identity, to qualify what the contemplative life is, yet identity does not connote a madness that makes a person falsely identify with some great character of history.

Identity, to be one with God, different from relationship to God, unfortunately leaves one with a sense of being religiously alone in the universe—with, of course, many wonderful people and companions—people with whom to worship and play, to love and to fight, to rejoice and to join with in sorrow. But God, for me, has never been one of those primary and significant persons who people my

Barbara Doherty

days. God has been around my life and within it, but never as a personal Other with whom I can carry on a conversation or to whom I can address prayers or whom I can call upon to pay the bills. Which is, oddly enough, not to say, "There is no God," though the experience of identity is so near to the experience of an atheism that one moves into this darkness with trepidation, fear and the haunting question of whether or not one has bungled life badly.

In very practical terms for those who read this and claim to know the experience about which I am struggling to speak, the contemplative experience of God is frequently an experience of NOTHING. Nothing is not an experience of SOMETHING. Nothing is nothing. I cannot state this strongly enough. When people read mystical literature, the nothingness experience may sound like something dramatic, inviting and wonderful. In truth it is an experience of NOTHING, just that, nothing. It is about as close to a no-God experience as a human can come who is at once a believer, a church-goer, a worshipper and a pray-er.

This godly experience is such a strange combination of nothing and everything *(todo y nada)* that to write of it, as I am forced to do here, sounds confused and foolish even to me. I beg the reader's sympathy. So fearsome an experience is this nothing and so gingerly does one walk this path, that a critical word throws one into an agony of questioning over again what is questioned daily.

It was in my early twenties, that I recognized that the way most people talked about God and experienced God was not the way I did. I sat through many retreats in which either in person or in my head I fought the retreat director every step of the way. I had no idea at that time why I was struggling. I only knew that the words I heard and who I was did not in any way match. For providential reasons, I guess I always had enough self-possession as well as an occasional mentor who would arrive just when needed to restore self-confidence to me as I pursued a path that was not named by any religious words which I heard.

I remember a retreat given by a superior of my congregation, a woman revered for her kindness and holiness of life. I found her words about the Divine so utterly opposite from anything that was a part of me, that I truly felt I had to abandon my life as a Sister of Providence. I revered this woman, yet I could not take her religious language into my life. Who was I to argue with a whole religious community and its respected leader, a woman respected by me as well? Gracefully, there was another middle management sister who counseled me to stay the course. I did. Many years later, I could put words to what was occurring in me at the time.

For whatever reasons, in the Providence of God, I was being led by the Spirit to a way of dealing with religion and the things of religion that has radically shaped who I am today. I now know I was being addressed about God by persons whose experiences of God were different from mine. Not better, not worse, simply different. I could not comprehend what they were talking about and they with great love and grace, though perhaps uncomprehending, loved me and allowed me to walk, however unsteadily, on a pathway that was confirmed only occasionally by an itinerant lecturer, a book or an event. Now many years later, I am able to see that my experiences were not at all unusual and that there are many women and men who know exactly what I am talking about. Ultimately, I wrote my book about the contemplative experience of God (for that is the name I knew to give to the process) probably as much for my own sake as to comfort and clarify for others the directions in which the Divine was leading. For instead of being odd or singular, contemplatives are everywhere, in every walk of life. They have lived in all times and places and continue to appear in our midst.

Hindus speak of three ways to approach the Ultimate; the way of devotion, the way of action and the way of knowledge. It is the latter that is the contemplative way, an interior, profound and far-reaching scope of knowing. This way to God is not a head trip nor does it preclude devotion or action. It does suggest, however, that the contemplative most easily "knows," in the broadest sense of the word, and that it is a knowledge that is not usually manifested in devotional feelings nor founded upon religious activities.

The hierarchical church has acknowledged the contemplative tradition, though not always with approbation. These spiritual knowers of many centuries had written and spoken of their experiences, yet perhaps because they attempted to articulate the non-relational quality of their experiences of God or struggled to make effable the ineffable, they seemed somehow different at best or, God forbid, gnostic at worst. They certainly did not figure prominently in the piety of the last 40 years in the churches, whether Protestant or Catholic.

It was among these contemplatives, however, that I found my spiritual friends and acquaintances. Scripture study, too, had verified for me the activity of God as found not in direct godly interventions in people's lives but in those persons or events that reveal God's presence. Thus the God who is radically immanent to history, mine and all others', became my God. "You shall be filled with all the fullness of God" is the text from Ephesians that most nearly describes the identity experience as different from one of relationship: "You shall love the Lord your God with your whole heart, your whole mind, and your whole strength."

So I was mysteriously set on this course. I know this action was a divine doing apart from any clever choices on my part. Is there a reason for it? At this juncture, I can only state that I have been able to be a spokesperson for the knowers and perhaps have been able to clarify to others what has been clarified to me by some gracious Providence. This contemplative posture has shaped and characterized the entirety of my life. Each day leads deeper into the darkness or into the mystery while yet each day holds other revelations that cause daily details to fall into place.

Non-believers will declare the whole business shaped by my psychological upbringing. So be it. Grace has always presumed nature and built upon it, at least according to the scholastics.

What is this mysterious knowing? It is certainly a worrisome business and it sounds arrogant. Indeed, to be gnostic is even less definable in Catholic circles than to be agnostic. Add to these predicaments that one must discuss gnostic with words like unknowing or darkness which certainly don't indicate rational discourse.

The knowing about which I write must be put into a faith category. The knowing is a faith knowing not a knowledge knowing. It is a knowing profound and strong which yet leaves many questions unanswered: Who is God? Where is God? How is God? Is there eternity? Those questions are placed on back burners of the mind and the fundamental knowing clung to: There is God and God acts within history, my own and all others. Having enounced this latter faith statement, the knower journeys in darkness and ambiguity with a clarity, nonetheless, that is profound and certain. Re-read the last sentence. How can a knower explain knowing with a sentence that abandons logic? It is faith-knowing that is described and it allows assurance/ambiguity and clarity/darkness to stand side by side in a balance, a proper stance, and in a god-given posture which is peace-bearing. I turn to some practical life details and move away from paradox at least for a while.

The prayer of the nothing experience has been called by traditional writers, the prayer of silence. The phrase perhaps reads like a state, wonderful and strange, to be hoped for because of its power and presence. However, the prayer of silence is similar to the nothing: there is silence—silence unbroken with feelings of fond devotion or unenlightened by sharp or clear insights other than those that would normally arise within a life given to examination and reflection, and that, within the time constraints of a person who normally works a 12 to 14 hour day.

In the time that is billed as personal prayer or reflection time, the nothing swallows me up. I have no thoughts, no words, no visions, no feelings, I just am. I am not displeased by the experience. It is normal. The biggest struggle is not to regard the silence as that state which occurs because I have not done my religious homework or put in the time that "good praying" might require. I have had to turn aside guilt feelings and trust my experiences over and over again. It is harder to do this when all around one the language of relating is spoken. I have often asked whether relationship/love will be the culmination of life or whether identity/confirmation will be the final state. I am comfortable leaving the outcome to divine dispensation.

Scriptures speak only rarely. I know the content and message only too well. I harbor thoughts that if I dedicated more time to reading the Word that it would reveal relationship to me. I return to scripture often only to find it a dried riverbed for me. I have had to learn to set scriptures aside with patience and belief that where and how I am led is godly and to be trusted.

I must note, however, differences in me in terms of common prayer and the worship of the assembly. I read somewhere that those who are thinkers, as tested by a Jungian instrument (Myers-Briggs), move with alacrity into common prayer and worship. Here, the feeling and enthusiasm of the faithful carry the thinker into the realms of movement and devotion not found when we grind away at our time of personal prayer and sit there hopelessly alone praying in the dark. Assured, yes. Ebullient, no.

In common prayer and liturgy, words, songs, ritual, ceremony, tradition all are assembled in richness, meaning and outward display. It is in common worship, I think, that I most often have an "a-ha" experience of understanding and clarity. The scriptures reveal new richness. Words and meaning leap off pages in song and preaching. In texts and symbol. And again, I know, oh yes, I know—often with tears of joy, relief, belief and new directions.

I surely see clearly why I can't understand people who "don't go to church." For me, worship is life and revelation. Though I can complain with the best of us about outward signs that are often imperfect compared to inward grace, still for me the faith at worship leaps over most chasms of tedium, as the power of word and sacrament carries me for a time away from the arid and the mundane.

I urge students of all faiths to go to church. I try to listen with sympathetic ear to Catholic feminists who have made a choice to stay away from worship, yet I understand clearly why I could never make the same decision. Perhaps feelers and those who live life with sturdy ties of relationship to the Divine can go it alone at home. Not so, me. Community is a must. People of faith struggling in the day-to-day gathered to sing their faith, offer peace to one another and stand together in the world for good, give me a strength I cannot do without. I look around at them and marvel at these ordinary women and men, believers all, committed to God and the things of God with a kind of simple purpose. I know they're all over the ball field in their theologies; I even know they are assembled for a multitude of reasons. Still they're there—believing, praying, singing and complaining—God's people, all. I love them; I wish

them well. I want to journey with them because together
we can have a consolidation of purposes and a common
attitude of strength as we walk the same pilgrimage to a
destiny known and unknown.

The classics of mysticism have become another group
of friends to me because I have discovered in these writings,
women and men who speak my language and who afford
me great comfort in believing I have not lost my wits, spiritual or otherwise. With Teresa, the Catherines, Bonaven-
ture, Gregory of Nyssa, the author of *The Cloud* (a woman
perhaps?) and many others, I explore the Alone and the
One. And I find my faith growing stronger rather than
weaker not because of visions or insight, but because of
companions and strength and explanations which find a
"yes" within me. I am confirmed along the dark path
again. I can trust nothing as indeed the godly situation in
which it is right for me to be.

A Christian believer can hardly conclude an essay on
"God and Me" without addressing the Jesus question. Who
is Jesus for me? Jesus is the One who I am being brought
to become. This faith declaration is not peculiar to contemplatives; in my understanding, it is the journey's end
for all Christian people. Baptismal theology has indicated
this outcome to us for centuries. I'm not certain why so
many people get stuck at the "relating-to-Jesus" stage. Jesus
is friend, guide, brother and companion. Perhaps to become Jesus has seemed somehow an extraordinary claim.
It is, however, the eventuality of the Christian's journey:
"It is now no longer I who lives...but Jesus...."

It is obvious that since the relational category has always

proved an obstacle for me, the identity category emerges again as the Jesus question is posed. I am to become Jesus. That simple answer is my religious direction. I have been in dialogic situations where my, "I am to become Jesus," language has been challenged. "Insert 'like,' " say the challengers. "You don't mean 'become Jesus,' you mean 'become like Jesus.' " No, I don't. I mean, forcefully and accurately, that the vocation of the Christian in the world is to become Jesus. Why is the assertion so oddly suspect? Does it put too great a demand on the Christian while the language of relating allows someone outside me to care for me and save me? Does the declaration of identity with Jesus take away a savior? Certainly not, but we are hampered in our ability to talk about being saved while simultaneously declaring becoming Jesus. The language seems to preclude saving unless one can grasp that the becoming is the saving. To make a case for being saved, using the language of identity, takes some effort. I make this effort for all who feel "outside the pale" of what is verbally comfortable and customary.

To be Jesus in the world means that I must become God's will as Jesus did, whatever the personal cost. It is only by my/our becoming Jesus again throughout history that the world is redeemed and is less a place of terror and confusion for humankind. In the day to day, this means that without fanfare and aggrandizement, there are people on the earth whose lives speak a godly message of assurance of purpose, expansion of religious insight and genuine and truthful receptivity to the friend and the stranger.

Thus, "to be saved" means that through all life's complex detail, confusion, and very often utter evil done by genuine evildoers, I have been empowered, renewed, indeed saved and raised up as God raised up Jesus. By my Baptism I am made daughter as Jesus is son. Divinity (and I can only catch a glimpse of whatever divinity is because of Jesus' saying, "When you see me, you see God,") is wedded to humanity once again in me as it is in Jesus. The harmonization of the opposites in the ordinary events of each day is the saving.

The use of the word "wedded" brings to mind that "mystical marriage" has frequently been a metaphor used by writers to explain contemplation. In my writing, I have used the symbol "integration" instead. Grace (the life of God) and nature (the life of me) are integrated by God's power and by my own choices and responses. This divinity/humanity integration is nothing peculiar, odd nor even an occurrence reserved to a few elect. The reconciliation of God and the human is the meaning of incarnation and salvation. This identity of divinity and humanity in human clothing both in Jesus and in the baptized, is the foundation of the Christian good news.

It has been the contemplatives of the tradition who have recognized such integration to be true not only for Jesus but in fact for us; for me, the writer of this chapter, and for you, the reader. I am brought to this integrity by God's power; thus, saved. Such salvation is God's intent and God's doing. The saving, however, occurs in all the ordinary situations of each day as I am saved from my own foolishness and stupidities and am brought to more profound integration of life and even to wisdom.

How ordinary is ordinary in which I am to catch a

Barbara Doherty

glimpse of salvation? I am challenged by someone in middle management who infers cryptically, or not so cryptically, that I don't know what I'm doing. Whether the manager is right or wrong, I must examine the critique and determine a course of action. I decide, I choose, I manage. I am convinced that all kinds of human situations (insert your own) are tied into the religious journey. By God's power, I live each day, usually never noting any divine presence. Situation after situation happens in the waking day. I listen, I think, I laugh, I cry. I visit, I fight, I love, I administer. In it all, I am saved as in it all, on rare occasions, I note a saving process as I view in hindsight a providential design, sometimes experienced as chaotic, sometimes as ordered. As I am chastened, refined and finely honed as a human being by the daily occurrences and as I reflect on these happenings with the scrutiny of the examined life and with faith, I can find myself becoming Jesus. Not because I've become so noble, gentle or magnanimous, but because I've died many times to my own small notions about reality, or perhaps not so small, and have been raised up/empowered by God once again. My life thus becomes a part of the Christic redemption repeated again in history in me.

Jesus causes to happen in me what by God's power happened in him. In scholastic definition we learned to refer to this occurrence as "exemplary causality." Jesus is the exemplary cause of my salvation. The sentence still makes wonderfully good sense to me even these many years after studying in Latin the *Summa Theologica* in my early theology classes.

With all of these fine and astute explanations, I am again

left at the end of this essay without a divine companion for my days. On certain rare occasions, however, revelation occurs for me. I have learned to wait for these revelations in faith, quietly, patiently knowing my way. I contrast waiting in faith with demanding futilely that my path be clarified by a constant divine presence. In fact, my life is clarified, by an occasional and welcome revelation of power and presence.

I have a treasured medallion which I purchased in Ireland. It is inscribed with the familiar swirls of traditional Celtic symbol. One of the illustrators of *The Book of Kells* fashioned the swirls into three separate yet interrelated circles. I hold the medallion in my hand and call out in the darkness, the words of the eighth century: "I bind to myself this day the power of the Trinity." And I know, for a few brief moments, presence and power—ever ancient and ever new. I know it to be so. I know it to be so.

Contributors

KAYE ASHE, O.P. is prioress general of the Sinsinawa
Dominicans. Born in Chicago, she lived in Europe for more
than a dozen years. In her early years there she earned a
doctorate in history at the University of Fribourg. She has
been particularly active in the women's movement. Her
book *Today's Woman, Tomorrow's Church* (1983) merited
the Thomas More medal for "an outstanding work of Catholic non-fiction". She lectures widely on topics related to
women in historical scholarship, women and spirituality,
and theological dimensions of the women's movement.

EDWIN CHASE, in Plimpton-like fashion, has incorporated several careers into half a century of living: naval of-
ficer, university professor, artist, corporate executive, and,
not least of all, writer. His writings sometimes reveal the
anguish of modern man, but as often as not the wry wit
of an S. J. Perelman, who, too, had his moments of anguish. A middle-westerner, he has lived in different parts
of the world. Like J. D. Salinger, he enjoys the life of a
recluse.

As a junior in high school, MAUREEN DALY had her first
short story "Sixteen" published in the *O'Henry Collection
of Best Short Stories* (1938). As a senior at Rosary College,
River Forest, Illinois, her first novel *Seventeenth Summer*,

was published. She has been writing ever since. Early literary success has lengthened into lifelong success. The main characters of her last novel, *Acts of Love*, are based on her husband (the late William McGivern) and daughter. Of it she says, "The book is my tribute, my way of holding on to the memory of Megan's and Bill's voices, their pleasures, their smiles of surprise. It is my way of keeping us together a little longer."

JOHN DEEDY is a veteran editor of the Catholic press. In his earlier years, he was on the staffs of diocesean newspapers in Worcester, Massachusetts and Pittsburgh. Then for many years he was managing editor of *Commonweal*. His articles have appeared in *The New York Times, The Critic, The New Republic*, and other journals. The author of many books, his two most recent are *My Aging Parents* and *The Catholic Fact Book*. This latter is widely used as a reference tool. He holds degrees from Holy Cross College and Trinity College, Dublin, and a certificate from the Institut du Pantheon. Mr Deedy now lives in Rockport, Massachusetts with his wife, Mary.

BARBARA DOHERTY, a member of the Sisters of Providence, is President of St. Mary-of-the-Woods College. She holds a Ph.D. in theology (with a specialization in the field of Asian religions) from Fordham University. She is the author of two books, *I Am What I Do: Contemplation and Human Experience* and *Make Yourself an Ark*. The former

GOD AND ME

outlines an apostolic spirituality and treats of what she sees as the very ordinary nature of religious experience. The thesis of the second work is that the journey to knowing self is the pathway to knowing God.

NORBERT F. GAUGHAN is Bishop of the diocese of Gary, Indiana. Prior to that he was Auxiliary Bishop of Greensburg. He earned his Ph.D. in philosophy from the University of Pittsburgh and for more than a dozen years was a lecturer in philosophy at its Greensburg campus. In the words of one literary pundit, "He's a bishop who reads." He also writes—and writes very well. His writings include regular newspaper columns and articles and reviews in theological journals as well as *Commonweal, Sunday Visitor* and *The Critic.* He is the author of *Shepherd's Pie* (1978) and *Troubled Catholics: Lessons from Discontent* (1988).

ROBERT C. MARSH has been a doctor of Harvard University for 37 years. He is best known as music critic of the Chicago *Sun-Times,* a job he has held since 1956 (and does superbly well). He was active as a college teacher in the 1940's and 50's and confronted the problems of combining scientific knowledge with humanistic values. He was briefly on the research staff of the Harvard Physics Department, and later, work in the philosophy of science was conducted at Oxford and at Trinity College, Cambridge. He has edited the early mathematical and logical papers of his most influential teacher, Bertrand Russell.

GOD AND ME

MARTIN E. MARTY is the Fairfax M. Cone Distinguished Service Professor of the history of modern Christianity at The University of Chicago and senior editor of *The Christian Century*. He is also president of the Park Ridge Center, an institute for the study of health, faith, and ethics. Marty has written about forty books, including—a propos this book's topic—*A Cry of Absence*. Of him *Time* magazine has said, "Wide ranging in his interests, lively in his prose and incisive of opinion, Marty, a Lutheran clergyman, is generally acknowledged to be the most influential living interpreter of religion in the U.S."

BERNARD J. RANSIL earned a Ph.D. in physical chemistry at Catholic University and his M.D. from the University of Chicago. Following completion of his M.D., he was a Guggenheim Fellow. He is an associate professor of medicine, Harvard Medical School, at Beth Israel Hospital, where he functions as a research consultant and analyst. He is the author of more than eighty scientific papers; he has also the gift of writing in a popular fashion. His profile of Robert Mulliken, 1966 Nobel laureate in chemistry, is his most recent article in the scientific field. It appears in *Dictionary of Nobel Laureates in Chemistry*. He is the editor of Mulliken's scientific memoirs to be published by Springer-Verlag.

MARTHA VERTREACE is a poet and an assistant professor of English at Kennedy-King College in Chicago. She

GOD AND ME

grew up in Washington, D.C., the child of a mother who was Cherokee and Black, and a father whose parents were German and African. She received a master of arts degree from The University of Chicago where she became a Catholic. Her first volume of poetry, *Second House from the Corner*, was published in the summer of 1986. Spoon River Poetry Press is the publisher of her second collection, *Artist Proof*, and Stormline Press will publish her third collection, *Entering the Dream*.